BOOKS BY DEBORAH DIGGES

Fugitive Spring

Deborah Digges

A MEMOIR

Fugitive Spring

NEW YORK
ALFRED A. KNOPF
1992

THIS IS A BORZOI BOOK
PUBLISHED BY ALFRED A. KNOPF, INC.

Copyright © 1991 by Deborah Digges

*In the process of completing this manuscript, I've heard many voices besides my
own, correcting and editing. I've taken liberties when it came to re-creating dialogue
and setting. Now and then I've collapsed time, invented details. If there are
mistakes, they're mine. Fugitive Spring is a version of a story. I wanted to write it
while we are, most of us, alive.* D.D.

Library of Congress Cataloging-in-Publication Data

Digges, Deborah.
    Fugitive spring : a memoir / by Deborah Digges. — 1st ed.
      p.   cm.
    ISBN 0-394-57722-1
    1. Digges, Deborah—Biography—Youth. 2. Poets, American—20th
century—Biography. 3. Jefferson City (Mo.)—Social life and
customs. I. Title.
PS3554.I3922Z464   1991
811'.54—dc20
[B]
                               91-52729
                               CIP

Manufactured in the United States of America
First Edition

FOR HARRY AND KATHLEEN FORD

CONTENTS

vii

Contents

Fugitive Spring

"I woke up this morning, and as I was getting up
and washing, everything on earth seemed
suddenly so clear to me. I knew how life should
be lived."

IRINA, *Three Sisters*

CHAPTER *1* NESTS

Every August the inmates from the prison farm crossed the bridge into town to pick apples for us. About forty men arrived in a green bus near eight each morning, guards as well as prisoners, and unloaded behind the house where my mother had set up under the twin mimosas a coffee machine and paper cups and doughnuts from the A & P. The younger men had a checked, vindictive vitality that came directly through their eyes as if their constant squinting were intended to keep the light in, not out, and they grinned often, for no apparent reason. The Wren's Farm inmates were thieves and vagrants mostly, off the small farms across the river or up from the Ozarks, where their people ran amusement stands and concessions—though it was a lean business during the fall and winter: places like Max Allen's Reptile Gardens, which you might have seen, in fact you couldn't miss if you've ever driven south on Highway 54.

Max Allen's is a huge stucco garage on the front of which is painted in swirling greens and grays and yellows a Rousseau-like jungle, but with the heads of snakes and lizards and Gila monsters turned snarling toward you. We went to see it once, and after paying, we were ushered into a dimly lit warehouse along whose walls were stacked many wire-mesh cages, most of them empty. In the ones that were not empty—and it was hard to tell, since they all had dirty straw lining the bottoms and most were high up and difficult for a child to see into—a few black snakes, local cottonmouths, and copperheads were burrowed under or coiled in a corner. Some of the cages had faded postcards attached showing a jungle snake hanging from a tree limb or devouring a monkey, its tail and hind end protruding. Above the cages on the cinder-block walls were water-spotted, shit-stained pictures, like sideshow posters, of Indians with flutes coaxing boas out of straw baskets, or, swooning in a trance, holy men with a snake or two wrapped around their neck.

Out back, and we hurried to escape the stink, there was a shallow pool, fed by a garden hose, at the center of which looked to be a paint-splashed rock. When the attendant prodded it, it moved, slowly raising its head, and, squinting in the sunlight, climbed onto the dirt. It was a tortoise who bore his name, Methuselah, in chipping graffiti across his wide carapace. As he moved deftly, dragging his huge shadow toward the pile of rotting vegetables the attendant had dumped on the ground, we were amazed at his sudden liveliness. He had looked only moments ago to be part of the inanimate, summer-burnt landscape, the dusty yard, the treeless bluffs shelving the Osage. He hissed as we approached as though *this* were the way a rock could sing. Galápagos tortoises don't have the beaky appearance of American turtles. Methuselah's mouth looked punched in and gave him a human aspect, like the weather-brown faces of the toothless old farmers who used to come into town on Saturdays for haircuts or to pick up supplies. We could ride Me-

4

thuselah, the attendant told us, for two dollars, but we declined. We just stood around awhile, staring, trying to get close enough to pat his shell. Then we walked sun-blind through the warehouse to the car.

The older men from the prison farm were in the minority. They looked to be in their fifties and sixties and had been wards of the state for many years, some of them finishing up sentences begun in the penitentiary for armed robbery or manslaughter. They held positions above the younger men, like foremen, sometimes giving an order or recording how many bushels to a tree; they rarely spoke and ignored us entirely, and the younger men steered clear of them. Across the bridges of their tight-skinned noses and along their cheekbones you could see dark sprays of keratoses from years and years in the sun. Sometimes my father, on his way to make rounds at the hospital, would stop to examine their faces and arms, and if anything looked suspicious, he'd take them, along with a guard, down to his clinic, where he'd burn off the potentially cancerous lesions. When the men came back to work, their arms and faces would be dotted with a white salve. Among the group, we knew of a father and son, and they spoke to each other once in a while, but like wolves that, sniffing one another, growl, then go their way as suddenly. We also knew of two brothers who stuck close together and whose names were Bobby-Lee and Billy-Lee. I approached them once to tell them that was my middle name too.

When a thing happens many times in a context that is as distracting as an orchard in late August—alive in all parts of itself—it's harder to remember that thing than if it had happened only once, as if the object that is memory could be erased by what it seeks to remember. But in the afternoons when it could get hot, say over a hundred degrees, the prisoners would line up at the pump and put their heads under the water, careful with one hand to hold on to their caps, and with the other hand cupped as much as they could and drank and spit and splashed the water down the backs of their shirts. This was their brief siesta, and for a few minutes they could lie in the shade and doze, eat a few apples or play with the dogs and tease us— always cautiously, shooting glances at the guards as they spoke—while we stood shy and staring and pleased to have them there, just as we were pleased when the Sisters of St. Mary's walked each spring through the orchard to admire the blossoms or when the Salvation Army came in the fall to pick cooking apples out of the weeds under the trees. Uniforms of all kinds excite children, maybe because they suggest secret adult rituals. The inmates wore drab green shirts and trousers, like army fatigues, and shapeless hats they had to wear all day by the rules. Lounging under the dusty green leaves made domestic with apples or against the smooth bark like elephant hide or standing halfway up a ladder with the sky behind them, they looked to belong there, and some of them came back to help us year after year, to harvest apples during the orchard's best time.

My two oldest brothers ran the orchard in the fifties. Everett was eleven years older than I, and seventeen years older than the youngest member of our family, so there was quite an age spread between us, six girls and four boys. For Everett the orchard seemed like a sentence he had to carry out each summer. He would rather, I think, like to be remembered riding in on his motorcycle with a road burn and bugs smashed across the part of his face not covered by goggles. But my brother Paul appeared to love the discipline that the orchard demanded. In the years that he ran it, it thrived.

The orchard was at best barely manageable. Many of the trees were old, even when we moved in in 1950, my birth year, and they required as much care as the younger trees. Insects and fire blight were constant problems. Fire blight is a disease that ruins the fruit with tiny reddish scales or "burns" that crawl across the surfaces and look, at first, like continents forming on a globe. Paul sprayed the orchard every three weeks or so, systematically covering the trees with parathion, which he pumped through the fire hose he'd rigged to an ancient spoke-wheeled drum. He pulled it, tree to tree, with the Allis-Chalmers. Parathion has recently been discovered to be a deadly toxin. In those days it was considered harmless, and none of us were poisoned. Paul treated the trees with a fine mist that looked like a dusting of snow, and when the apples came they were treated too, and we picked them green and wiped them on our shirts and ate them where we stood.

The word *wilderness* can be traced back to the Anglo-Saxon *wylder* and *ness*, or "wild nest, the place of the heathen." From these comes our word *bewilderment*, which means "knowing the true fragility of order." The orchard was a little wilderness full of opossums and rabbits, skunks, woodchucks, box turtles, black snakes, toads, lizards, raccoons, and other small life. Once we had a Siamese cat who disappeared for longer and longer periods of time until he went completely wild and would hiss and spit if we tried to approach him. In the end he would no longer respond to his name and we grew afraid of him and left him alone, but now and then we'd catch sight of him in a tree or in the tall grass around the pond. He'd grown huge on rats and mice and birds, his originally light tan markings now a deep brown, almost black, and he would look at us with contempt as he eased off his perch or slunk away through the weeds. No doubt, in our bumbling, we'd scared away his prey.

In keeping with ancient, medieval, and Middle English art

and literature, John Milton called Genesis's tree of knowledge an apple tree. Among the many stories Milton knew, each in its original language, the apple figured in the Greek myth of Eris, goddess of discord, who found a particular golden apple to be the most beautiful. Later, Paris, son of the king of Troy, offered this fruit to Aphrodite, who returned the favor by helping Paris kidnap Helen. So began the Trojan War. There is also mentioned in ancient Hebrew writings the story of the Dead Sea apples, which Josephus describes as "very beautiful, as if they were fit to be eaten, but if you pluck them with your hands, they dissolve into smoke and ashes." Milton's word and ours, the Latin *Pyrus Malus*, has come to mean not only the edible fruit of a tree, but also anything of promising appearance which disappoints or deceives.

And yet what is it particularly about the apple that it has been so invested with the idea of beauty, of godlike knowledge, invested, therefore, with the notion of human weakness, primarily greed, which is the first of the seven deadly sins? If you gave a man gone blind a peach, and then a pear, and then an apple, why would he choose the last? Of the three, the peach's shape is the most perfectly global. Its surfaces are the most fleshlike and sensual, and its pit may be the most femininely sexual object in nature. And why not the pear with its form connoting ripeness, fullness, like the last days of pregnancy, which has been painted many times on the walls of tombs and on the sarcophagi that are carved like boats to carry the dead into Paradise?

But the apple is the most tactilely strange and various of all, and solid, so that you trust it in your hands, its smooth surfaces suggesting a brightness beyond its "colors mixed ruddy and gold." As far as you can force your finger into the funnel at the stem, the skin feels grainy, blighted, while on the opposite side a series of irregular mounds protrude, like the bones in a face, around a little dust that was the blossom. There are five seeds in every apple. Milton was going blind when he began *Paradise Lost*, and as the story goes, he held an apple in his hand as he spoke, as his daughters wrote furiously. Did he know that if you cut an apple horizontally, severing the seeds, each half shows a perfect five-pointed star?

A surprising variety of birds nested, usually three and four times a season, in our trees. Particular kinds of birds are attracted to apple orchards, robins and kingbirds, especially, and chipping, field, and song sparrows, among others of that species, along with jays, waxwings, cardinals, orioles, and wrens, and in the early spring, redwing blackbirds that nested in the cattails around our pond. The apple tree is a factor in perpetuating these and other species, not only because of the fruit that feeds them, but because of other kinds of life an apple tree propagates— insects and worms and a variety of molds, and, when the fruit rots, different kinds of protein and bacteria which help both the migrators and the winter inhabitants to store energy.

Bees love apple orchards and we kept four domestic hives though we knew of other wild hives in the surrounding woods. The years we had plenty of rain and all the trees blossomed and the wood roaches left them alone and the apples came faster than we could pick them, the honey of those harvests would be a light golden color. You could hear it all night in the kitchen coming easily and steadily through the linen, a huge pendulum of crushed combs which hung over a washtub and which grew smaller and smaller as the jars filled, this lightest harvest like the honey of Paradise. But the years we had little rain and late freezes that killed the blossoms and stunted the crop, the grass, the wild flowers that bloomed pale and spiny, the honey of those harvests would be a dark, rich brown, and more viscous, and it would stain the linen as my mother, wearing only her slip in the heat, kneaded and kneaded the combs, but it would not come through easily.

Once Siegfried tasted the heart of a dragon and knew suddenly the language of birds. Eve tasted the apple and "rearranged the cosmos generally." What a strange and exhausting burden must have seemed this new godlike need for order that Eve would cultivate after *the fall* as she cleared away weeds, waited for the sky to clear or cloud, for the droughts to end or the floods recede, or for the child inside her, grown, it must have seemed, to a terrible size, to be born. By the consequence of her sin the cortex inside the fetus she carried doubled daily. The head, finally so painfully lodged, then passed, still grew, even as Cain breathed. Man is the only mammal whose offspring's brain continues to grow until well into the first years. If a human baby were as well developed at birth as an ape baby, for instance, it would be much too large to deliver. The number of deaths of mothers in human childbirth is greater than in any other mammal, as Stephen J. Gould tells us in *Ever Since Darwin*. Milton knew something about this. He lost two wives as they delivered his daughters. It was as if, by Eve's sin, she had unlocked the brain's casings. Now she could feel her son's heart beat in two places, in his chest, and lightly, like wing flutterings, on the fontanel.

We grew Jonathans and Winesaps and red and yellow Delicious and Henry Clays on sixteen acres that sloped gradually into a huge, comfortable lap. If you balanced on top of the swinging gate in the late fall after the trees had lost their leaves and ground had been cleared and burned, you could see that once there had been an order. Once the trees had been planted in neatly spaced rows with the skeleton of a grape arbor on the east slope behind which you could glimpse the barn's blue roof that matched the roof of the house to the west. You could see into and through the trees to the flat November sky that would hardly change now through winter. And you could see all the dead nests, more than you ever imagined in summer, their sudden visibility like clues to history. Now you could climb to them and dislodge them and examine them for strands of your own hair sewn together with grass and milkweed and dandelion down and pieces of drab green thread and, once, a piece of Christmas tinsel we called rain that shone against a mud base so firm it might have been baked in a kiln.

Michelet, who has written so beautifully about birds, calls a nest a bird's suffering. "There is not one of these blades of grass," he says, "that in order to make it curve and hold the curve, has not been pressed on countless times by the bird's breast, its heart, surely with difficulty in breathing, perhaps even with palpitations." This must be true for all products of genius. I had tried, as children often do, to draw a perfect circle, and now I was surrounded by hundreds, of different sizes and materials, made, without hands, piece by piece, in over two thousand trips and maneuvers, out of the natural and the cast off, out of things dead and alive.

The life span of wild birds varies. The hearts of all mammals beat about the same number of times. Were we to understand our lives in other than lunar time, twenty-four hours a day, fifty-two weeks a year, we would see that all mammals live as long, as many heartbeats. If we apply this to other warm-blooded vertebrates, birds, for instance, it figures that some of the larger species, eagles and crows and pigeons, will live forty years, their hearts beating more slowly than the literal whir in the breasts of the robins and jays and waxwings, the sparrows and the wrens which live maybe ten years, and which nested in our orchard. Some of them stayed through the winter and we fed them, when we remembered, from leftover bacon rinds and bread heels—if the dogs didn't get to them first—and some of them migrated according to their own circadian rhythms as the days got shorter and colder and there was nothing left now of the apples or the insects or the rot that had yielded them the last of the seeds. "And five of you shall chase one hundred," says the prophet in Leviticus, "and one hundred of you shall put ten thousand to flight."

CHAPTER 2 THE LAB

Cleaning the rat cages was a dreaded job. In my father's laboratory next to the house were four floor-to-ceiling wire-mesh bureaus, five or six drawers in each. As many as a hundred rats were kept in the cages, and about three times a month their fouled shavings must be emptied and replaced, their food supplies replenished, and their water bottles scrubbed and refilled. They were the albino pink-eyed variety—mutations of the Norway rat—bred for their delicate immune systems which in many startling ways resemble humans'. Drawer by drawer the rats must be transported to holding cages. You had to open each section slowly, taking care not to catch a paw or a tail between runners, then quickly, lest one escape, herd them into a corner.

They always protested, the big males rearing on their haunches and baring their teeth before they ran to the back or tried to leap over the side. Then you must clap your hands or bang on the bottom of the drawer, terrorize them long enough to take hold of their tails and lift them, squealing and thrashing, through the air. The males could so profoundly arch their bodies, you were in danger of getting bitten, while the females, usually pregnant, hung so still you took to moving them one at a time, supporting their bodies with your free hand all the way to the holding cage. Or if you came on a new nest, you could leave that drawer alone, only freshening the shavings while the mother rat cowered over her young or darted back and forth, the litter falling from her teats.

The rats were the subject of an ongoing research project which my father carried out alone through the fifties and sixties as he studied new approaches to treatments and possible cures for cancer. Through an intricate system of reproduction and trans-plantation of tumors, he kept his rat population stable, working nights and weekends on various investigations that would lead him to discover, for instance, that certain kinds of cancer are organ specific—that is, cancer of the breast begins in breast tissue. Transplanted at an early stage to the bowel or stomach, it will not metastasize at the new site. It may, in fact, disappear, the new host simply rejecting it. This doesn't mean, however, that the cancer would not, of its own accord, eventually spread from the primary site to the lymph system and on to other organs. But the insight that particular organs are originally and only susceptible shed light on other things: the mysterious workings of the immune system, and by extension, heredity.

Of course the rats' mortality rate was high. During February and March each year, when things were slow at my father's clinic, he spent a good deal of time on his experiments, killing off as many as twenty rats a month. Then the ground was hard or under a few feet of snow, so he'd wrap the carcasses in plastic and store them in the lab's refrigerator, among his Cokes and diet drinks, toward a mass burial in the spring in one of our many and various gardens. Year after year as we tilled the soil we'd turn up tiny skulls which we slipped in our pockets, or more often, tails, which we left alone. And true enough those gardens thrived. We won blue ribbons at the Cole County Fair every August for our huge flower arrangements or summer squash or sweet corn, though we were hard pressed to eat the vegetables that grew so voluptuously out of that compost. When the green beans had been passed twice around the dinner table without our touching them, our father would laugh. "Hair of the dog." He'd wink at us and heap his plate high.

During the humid Missouri summers the rats required more frequent attention owing to the fact that the lab was half of a larger building. The other side, a garage, served as our apple showroom. Bushel baskets displayed on risers brimmed with red and yellow Delicious under a homemade sign that read ORCHARD ACRES. Behind the risers my brother Paul had set up a table on which he kept the cash box and an automatic coffee percolator and cups in case the customers, in spite of the heat, might like some coffee as they browsed. Left more than a week unattended, the rats' peppery urinous and fecal odors would seep under the door that connected the one room to the other and overtake the sweet, plastic smell of apples. Paul feared it would scare away our prospective buyers, who came, usually in the evenings after work, to select by the bushel or the peck. For those of us who wanted to share in the profits at the end of the summer, Paul set up a rat detail clean-up rotation which included not only our taking our turn in providing the rats with fresh shavings biweekly, but also emptying half a can of Apple Blossom deodorizer in the showroom each afternoon at about four, just prior to our heaviest business.

Not that the profits at the end of each summer were ever that great. During Paul's management of the orchard, the money we brought in by selling apples usually went right back into maintenance. One year we purchased a machine that actually sorted apples by size. Another year we bought some new extension ladders to make it easier for the prisoners to get to the fruit in the treetops. Still, we took our turns with the rats, mostly, I imagine, because we loved spending evenings in the showroom with Paul where we drank the acid coffee and polished apples past midnight with his secret weapon—beeswax cut with linseed oil—and listened to the stock cars revving and crashing a mile below us at the fairgrounds.

The bald showroom bulb threw out a net of light, say, ten feet into the dark and we liked to play at the periphery, hopscotching in and out of Paul's vision, calling his name or trying to get him to play hide-and-seek with us. Now and then he relented, put down his cloth, and leaning against the lab wall, began counting out loud. It was understood that he was always initially it, and usually we never got farther than that. In a dark like I've never known again, a dark thickened by the chlorophyll haze that smelled of the rats and coffee and apples and the river, it took Paul a long time to find us, Rena, Gena, Eva, Connie, David, Beth, Stevie, and me.

Or Paul would turn out the light and we'd lie down on the grass and watch for shooting stars. To see one meant that somewhere on the planet someone was dying, a notion, probably Dutch, which we took to be fact and accepted without question. All of us went, one summer Sunday morning or another, to St. Mary's Hospital with our father and Everett or Paul as they made their rounds of the patients, many of them terminally ill with cancer. We'd stand in the doorway while Paul pulled the little curtain around the bed and by our father's instruction, examined a man or a woman's fresh incision, or placing his hands on either side of the patient's neck, felt for swollen lymph glands, and the glands under the arms, the groin, the window light behind them widening as the sun came up, their shadows huge on the curtain as Paul asked tenderly, "Feeling bad?" Maybe the patient nodded. Then some night late the phone would ring. Even as the nine of us lay on the grass looking up at the Big Dipper, one of the nurses at St. Mary's listened for our father to answer. Two rings, three. We could hear it out the open upstairs windows. When it stopped we lay still.

Paul was, I think, for all eight of his younger siblings, the favorite brother, if for no other reason than because he took time with us. Everett was temperamental and distant. In fact I suspect I'm more like Everett. Maybe that's why I remember Paul this way. Nine years older than I and fourteen years older than our youngest brother, Stevie, Paul seemed not so turned always toward the future. Through college and medical school, while Everett toured the Middle East on the Harley he'd bought with money made moonlighting in the emergency rooms in New York City, Paul came home every summer to run the orchard. One year he also took a job preaching in a little church just outside Jefferson City.

How he came to get the job, I'm not sure. Maybe the congregation had lost its minister. Maybe he'd seen a notice in the local paper asking for a volunteer, or our own minister, Reverend Nelson, had taken Paul aside and enlisted his help. Of course Paul wasn't ordained. He was a medical student. But he had taken voice lessons and a course in public speaking at a small college in Jefferson City. Maybe that was enough to qualify him as a lay preacher in the eyes of the church elders. Paul was constantly trying to improve himself. Small for his age during his teenage years, he'd ordered barbells, leg and head weights from the Charles Atlas Catalog and had worked out daily, following carefully the mail order program until he'd built up his body. He even wore the neck weights—a kind of leather cap from which hung, like wilted laurels, iron disks—while he practiced the French horn; though in the end he in no way resembled the greased muscle men in the pictures. Rather, by his eighteenth year, as he gained height as well as weight, he developed a long graceful body which he'd soap up each evening at the kitchen sink, then let the white film dry on his skin to get, he'd claim, the full benefit of the cleansing.

Paul was a stickler for cleanliness and responsible for introducing his eight younger siblings to the unseen world of bacteria, in water, for instance. Once one of us toted a pickle jar of algaed murk up from the pond and Paul made slides of it in the lab, allowing each of us to view, through our father's high-powered microscope, a writhing horror. "They're everywhere," Paul pronounced a warning matter-of-factly, "whether you can see them or not. Remember to wash, now, and brush your teeth. And listen, stay out of the dogs' house. You could pick up ringworm in there." Paul breathed on the dissecting table glass and drew a circle in the fog to illustrate. "Watch out for it, OK?" Our hygiene improved those summers. Even the baby Stevie would no longer accept a piece of already chewed gum. He'd stoically decline the pink wad of Double Bubble one of us offered him. "I want new gum. Paul taught me germs."

Because I liked to sing, Paul let me accompany him to his new church on Sunday evenings to lead the choir, though week after week I'd lose my nerve as we drove the blacktop roads to the service. But Paul never made an issue of my shyness. Once we arrived at the church he'd simply do both—lead the singing and preach the sermon. His sermons were a little like lectures, different from the Southern Baptist approach the congregation was used to, which characteristically included the preacher's shouting about sin, interrupting himself dramatically as he'd sidle up to the congregation, walk among it shaming and coaxing. Paul stuck close to the podium, close to facts, history. I don't remember his lessons exactly, but it was like him to trace, for example, the periods of time the apostle Paul spent in prison. Or he might discuss the ongoing problems of translating biblical documents from the Greek, listing for the congregation—most of them farmers and their families—the names of all the texts from Gregory to Tyndale. His closing remarks went something like this: "Folks, let's take a minute here to contemplate salvation." Then the pianist would begin the hymns of decision, and surely Paul, in his dignity, won a few souls to Christ, the newly saved making their way to him calmly, modestly, like graduates.

CHAPTER *3* THE POND

The pond lay at the bottom of the orchard slope, a little to the east. It was about sixty feet across and at its deepest point, maybe fifteen feet. It was not fit to swim in nor did any of us really want to, because to get to the water you had to wade through a thick moss border that hosted, under a haze of gnats, its own reptilian life. If you pulled the moss out of the water, say, with the end of a stick, all sorts of creatures dove or flew off it—frogs and flies and water snakes and tadpoles— and there were hardly any fish in the pond because of several huge old snapping turtles. On summer afternoons my brothers used to try to tease one to the surface by dragging a branch across the shallows. Most of the time the snappers would ignore it and lie low, but once in a while we'd see the mottled ridge of a shell break water and a snapper would clamp fast to the branch and would not let go, even as it was lifted high into the air, the loose folds of its neck stretched tight as a fledgling's and its webbed feet rotating and its bright underside flashing as my brothers swung it mercilessly around, flinging pond water everywhere, faster and faster until they were pulled forward, themselves, by the inertia.

Cattails grew prolifically in the pond's several inlets. In the marshes we'd find the footprints of opossums and rabbits, and more and more frequently, as the woods around us were cut back and developed, the footprints of deer. Once in a while we'd discover the shell of a box turtle, and after we had let it dry out in the sun and the insects had picked it fairly clean, we'd scrub it with Clorox and water to get rid of any residue of carcass, and in the end it would be as white as plaster. A box turtle's shell is surprisingly heavy, about the arc and heft of a pottery bowl, even one as small as three inches in diameter. Cleaned and stripped of its brown- and yellow-flecked sheen, its surfaces feel sandy across the shallow indentations of the carapace, like something carved from stone. We set our turtle shells on our dressers and as we grew older we used them to hold our bobby pins and barrettes and rubber bands. One April my little sister filled one with bright plastic straw and placed foil-covered chocolate eggs inside.

When Charles Darwin rode the backs of the huge Galápagos tortoises on James Island where the *Beagle* had put down anchor, he was not yet an evolutionist. He was a young man, just over twenty, bound, he believed, for the ministry. He saw himself, like Milton, a little below the angels. "I found it very difficult," he'd report in his journals, "to keep my balance . . . These huge reptiles," he continued in his notes on Chatham Island, "surrounded by the black lava and leafless shrubs, and large cacti, seemed to my fancy like some antediluvian animals. The few dull colored birds cared no more for me than they did the huge tortoises." This entry, dated September 15, 1835, is a prophecy of sorts. The finches, later named Darwin's finches, which by the variety of the shapes of their beaks, and the tortoises, whose broad carapaces also varied island to island, were to be for Darwin the two primary examples of adaptation in the theory of evolution and the origin of species.

How far removed one April was the shell of that box turtle, now scrubbed and filled with eggs, from the surprisingly graceful little animal that had prowled the orchard looking for shade under the trees, drinking with startling dignity from the pond —raising its head to swallow—then crawling off into the autumn marshes under the cattails where it would die, as turtles often do, during hibernation. In this way a turtle's life and death may be the most transfiguring event in nature. Its shell was a nest on our Easter table.

When I was about eight I fell through the ice over the pond and nearly drowned. We had taken the tractor down, as we often did during the coldest months in Missouri, January and February, and my older brothers and sisters skated while we younger ones slid across the ice in our boots or lay down on the surface to look past the leaves, overlaid and magnified, and past the moss like green smoke circling the shallows, hoping, against the laws of hibernation, to catch sight of the snappers. This particular Sunday there was about a foot of snow on the ground but the sun was shining and the marshes were muddy and the ice pulpy so that if you jumped a little, a green ooze pooled around your boots. Since the pond lay at the bottom of a series of slopes, it was subject, through erosion, to landfill, and as the banks were extended year by year, the cattails grew more dense and shrank the pond's circumference until they had to be burned to the ground and their roots shoveled back.

My father and mother believed that they were distant cousins since they were both of Frisian descent, their families, the Dykstras and the Elsingas and the Mudds and the Van Dykes, coming from northern Holland, from the tiny isolated sea- and windswept Groningen, where over the centuries the chief occupation and concern was literally holding back the ocean, building and repairing the dikes. In the late 1800s each of their families had come to America by way of Ellis Island, my grandfather standing next to his father as the officials translated their name. Early springs my parents stood in hip boots in the pond shallows and attacked the burnt stubble, turned up huge clumps of earth and pitched the load behind them, as if some genetic intuition were at work, some blood-remembering beyond the specifics of time and place. They shoveled without speaking and seemed to be listening to something behind their own breath, pulse, the water sounds and the sucking sound of the roots as they were pulled away, listening, maybe, to some residual memory of a cold sea pounding, a cellar filling in the night. *Frisia non cantat*, reported Tacitus of the northern regions of Holland to the citizens back in Rome. "Friesland does not sing."

The burning and shoveling back of the cattails usually took place after the first thaws, but that January day, all ten of us skating or sliding across the ice which, sun-stricken, threw off a glare that nearly blinded, my father took the tractor back up to the house and returned with several gallons of gasoline. It ruined the cold winter smell of the day but the blaze was beautiful as it caught, weed by weed, until one half of the pond was surrounded by a hedge of fire through which you could glimpse the snowy hillside. It made a sound like wind or ocean surf so that I didn't at first hear my mother shouting for us to get off the ice. Then I heard only the panic in her voice as she watched me, the last one, who, in order to get to the shore not burning, had to come all the way across. When you walk on a wet beach watching the ground, you can see how the impact of your steps darkens a moment, leaving a puddle where your foot was. The ice gave under me in this way until it simply opened like a door. I don't remember being cold or afraid that I might die, but rather the way the sun looked from under the ice, like a dirty paper lantern over a weak bulb, and the sound of my voice under water, changed but familiar. I would try that again in the tub or hear it years later in dreams about my children when I was away from them. And I remember one other thing. Each time I grabbed for a hold, the ice came off in my hands, as though the ladder I climbed were sinking, rung by rung.

What happened after that has been told to me on occasion along with other family stories of near catastrophe. Mine's one of the less dramatic. Once while he was pruning our hedges my father cut off part of his index finger, but as a left-handed surgeon as skilled with his right, he sewed it back on at the kitchen table. That January day he came out on the ice on his belly and it did not give way under him. He reached down into the hole and pulled me out by my hair. I had a little cold afterward, my mother would say, but that was all. In the spring we found my boots floating like small boats on the pond.

Behind the pond railroad tracks bordered the south property line. The Missouri Pacific station was about three miles to the east of us, so the long freights had slowed by the time they passed our orchard and hoboes sometimes leaped from the boxcars and made camp down there. "Hobo" is strictly an American term that originated after the Civil War, and it refers to the men, mostly from the South, who had nothing to go home to and so took to traveling across the country, working at odd jobs or panhandling in the cities until they had enough money to last them awhile. Missouri was a border state, its citizens divided in their sympathies. The Civil War song about the two brothers marching off to war, one wearing a Union uniform, the other wearing Confederate gray, is a fact documented over and over in Missouri's war logs, and you can see it for yourself entered on cemetery headstones. When some of these men returned from the war, relations were strained and there was little money to run their farms. Many Missouri veterans went west, broke, hopping the trains, hiding behind the livestock and feed sacks until the engines took speed. Or they became outlaws. Frank and Jesse James, from western Missouri, had fought for the Confederate Army.

In the fall, when the harvest was over and all the equipment was locked up in the barn and we were sure it was going to be winter but instead warm weather came and we were outside again, all over the brown orchard, we'd find the smashed glass from the hoboes' Old Crow bottles and empty Van Camps bean cans and jerky wrappers and the char from their fires on the sandstone around the pond. Sometimes we'd find a piece of cloth, from a shirt, maybe, which my brothers guessed the hoboes had used to strain the moss from the water before boiling it, and once we found a pair of huge canvas shoes which we filled with stones and threw to the center of the pond.

We didn't know where the hoboes came from. Once in a while when my mother took us on the train to St. Louis to shop or visit the museums, we'd see men outside the station selling pencils or playing harmonicas and kazoos for money, and we looked hard at their clothing to see if it in any way resembled the piece or two we'd found; we wanted to speak to them, ask them if they'd ever camped in our orchard, but we were afraid. Some of those hoboes may have been veterans from the first and second world wars, but most were probably just drifters heading, each fall, to a warmer climate where they might find some work. In the evenings at bedtime we begged to be read Riley's "The Raggedy Man," because the character in that poem was a hobo like ours who must have greeted his companions, as legend has it, "Ho! Beau!" as if that's how they got their name.

We tried to make a fire like theirs on the sandstone with dry cattail reeds and leaves and apple wood, but we could never get it to burn. Finally it was our conclusion that the hoboes must first douse the wood with whiskey. Apple wood, unless it's been aged awhile, isn't much good for anything besides making apples. It's pulpy and so holds moisture long past its death and won't be, except by some secret, tricked into burning. It would rather rot. The sixteenth-century alchemist Paracelsus identified and studied the four basic elements. Bachelard later compared these to "the doctrine of the four temperaments in whose dreams fire, water, air, and earth predominate." Maybe the hoboes dreamed of fire. At least for us fire was their context—two or three of them squatting in the dark, Promethean in their solitude, their faces ruddy with alcohol, alive in the light. Loitering around the ashes in the season's weak warmth, we held pieces of the amber glass from their bottles in front of our eyes so that the orchard, in sepia, looked suddenly timeless, golden, and as the birds blurred in and out of our lenses, it was easy to see what the sky looked like from the open door of a moving train.

We never actually saw the hoboes, not one, nor the flames from their fires. In fact you couldn't surprise them, not by memorizing the train schedules or hiding past the first stars in a tree or waiting in the dark with binoculars at the third-story window, which was my brothers' room. All we ever knew of them is what we found. Even the crushed path through the goldenrod led us only to the tracks west to Kansas, Colorado, Wyoming,

New Mexico, California, and then the Pacific Ocean, and the hoboes were as real to us as that, and as mortal, and as faceless as the pennies we picked up again, Indian summer afternoons, from the rails.

What we did see on the pond in the early spring, if we were lucky, were sea gulls. This was rare and happened only in some years. They were easy to miss since the pond was some distance from the house. Our mother usually spotted them during a morning from an upstairs window as they rose and hovered and dove. Then we would creep down to the pond after school and most of the time we were disappointed, the surface as smooth as an empty dance floor. We'd accuse our mother of having mistaken them for the pigeons that roosted in the barn eaves. But one year we came on a dozen or more, some of them floating like white sails, others circling in the close sky above the circle of the pond. They'd come inland, probably from the Northeast, to feed on the algae that thrive after the thaws on rivers and lakes and ponds throughout Iowa, Illinois, and Missouri. A few of them perched awkwardly in the bare apple trees that lined the ridge along the tracks, and you could glimpse, as they shifted uneasily from one bright orange foot to another, the stained webs between their claws.

We'd seen ducks of all varieties, and at the lake nearby where we spent most of each summer, we'd lured them with bread close to our dock and after a while they'd become almost tame. One summer my brother Everett, hiding beneath the pilings, caught two ducks by coming at them underwater and grabbing their feet. Another time we came across a sick mallard on Lake Ozark's rocky shore and had built a little nest for her out of driftwood and weeds. If you live on a coast, gulls are to you as the ducks were to us. In this way years later I watched the natives of the South English coast move with uncanny calm through a day of violent and changing weather, wind, then rain, then bright sunlight, then suddenly rain again, and wind that blew the gulls hard against the huge, salt-oiled windows. But the natives didn't look up from their reading nor did they care to watch the gulls blown backwards by the gusts as though the earth had slowed to a halt and had begun turning now in the opposite direction. After a week in Devon I noticed that I, too, stopped watching the birds and my son stopped collecting their feathers.

But that day by our pond none of us had ever seen a coastline except on postcards or in books or in the stories our father told us about his childhood on the New Jersey beaches. The gulls' bright saltwater-born feet clutching the twiggy apple boughs and their heads like Egyptian royalty and their dead eternal gaze and their whiteness thrilled us. We didn't try to catch or feed them. We stood back a ways and tried not to move for fear of scaring them off. Among the tattered winter birds, the few starlings there, the sparrows, the gulls seemed to raise the ceiling of the sky, as if our boundaries had suddenly been extended to include an ocean, islands.

CHAPTER 4 STRAYS

One autumn in the late fifties a Wren's Farm inmate walked away from a work detail. Maybe he hid, that night, in one of the animal stalls in the government stockyards, or waited among the sandpiles at the concrete plant until it was dark, then crossed the river on one of the barges. Or maybe he just walked across the bridge. I don't think anyone ever asked him how he got to Jeff City, or where he got the gun. There wasn't anything about it in the papers. It's possible the police knew the answers, but thought better of sharing them with the public, as if those facts might scare the citizens, or give other inmates ideas. After all, Jefferson City was a prison town and the state capital. The Governor's Mansion stood only a little way upriver from the penitentiary. On the east edge of town, deep inside the penitentiary, was the gas chamber, from which the families of the condemned sometimes issued last-minute pleas. They'd appear on the ten o'clock news, most always the mothers or the wives. Or they'd stand with the reporter in front of the Governor's Mansion. "In these last hours," the reporter would say, "here at the eleventh hour . . ." since the executions always took place at midnight.

But the fugitive from the prison farm had never been in serious trouble. That's why he was at the farm and not in the penitentiary. He may have been a car thief, or a vagrant. He may have picked apples for us one summer or another. So that when he broke into a house down the road from us the next morning at dawn, broke in and held a man and his wife at gunpoint, tied them up, stole provisions, and escaped again, we couldn't understand why we weren't allowed to go out, except to school, and had to come home right after. It was autumn and warm. We liked to ride our bikes out Boonville Road into the country to what we called the haunted house, an old house the occupants had, some years back, simply abandoned. Nobody knew why. Maybe it had been part of a farm that failed.

My sister Gena liked to tell the story of how, when kids first discovered it was empty, they found the kitchen table set, down to a jar of pickles at the center. "It was like the people just walked out one day," she'd say. "The closets were full of clothes. There were even clothes on the clothesline out back, mail in the mailbox." "What else?" we'd ask, until we had a hunch she'd begun inventing details. Sometimes stray dogs had litters of pups there. Over the years, Gena brought home many pups from the haunted house. They didn't live long. The one she named Sputnik—the first Russian satellite had just gone up— had distemper even as she carried it home in her bike basket. Others were hit by cars. But the one that she named Peter Vigil survived several accidents. By the end of his first year his back leg was paralyzed, but he ran on three legs as fast as our other dogs. Pete was smart. Even our father said so. He was a cross between a beagle and a boxer, with a few other breeds thrown in. He often followed us to school, lounging on the front steps until recess. If the principal saw him, he'd call the dogcatcher. Pete learned to know that white truck and would take off into the woods at the sight of it, the children cheering him on.

Pete led our other dogs in chasing steers belonging to a man named Mr. Wilson whose farm lay beyond a wheat field to our left. When we spotted him coming up the hill between the rows we knew he meant to speak to our father about Pete. "I don't want my steers running," he'd say as he wiped his forehead with a handkerchief. Our father stood at our back door listening, his hands in his pockets. "I sell by the pound," continued Wilson. "The way I see it, that dog of yours owes me a bundle. I'm just warning you, Doc. If that dog comes around again, I'll shoot him." We knew, by the way Pete's spine swelled, that Wilson had already fired on Pete with a shotgun full of salt pellets. "We'll keep him tied up," our father would reassure Wilson, but in fact, one morning near dawn, our father put Pete in the car and drove him about forty-five miles south, almost to the lake, and let him out among several farms. He'd done this before with other strays, cats and dogs alike. "Somebody will begin feeding Pete," he promised us. "Then he'll have a whole farm to run on. And no one will shoot at him anymore." But that morning, when our father's car pulled into the driveway again, Pete was waiting at the back door to greet him. He panted triumphantly, his atrophied back leg wagging with his tail. The next morning our father took him west toward Sedalia, and the next, across the river, but Pete always beat him home. "Let him stay"—our mother laughed—"and take his chances." Pete lived to be nearly twenty years old.

Things would have quieted down quickly under ordinary circumstances, but the man whose house the inmate had chosen to break into happened to be a judge in Cole County. We'd come down to breakfast the morning after the inmate's disappearance to hear the judge's voice on the radio as he described the intruder. "Young fellow," he said, " 'bout six feet tall, I guess, brown hair . . . Looked scared. Didn't get away with much— a couple of cans of beans. I'm sure he couldn't have gotten far." The judge worried mostly about his wife, who'd been badly frightened. The broadcaster turned now to the public. "There's an all-out search in progress. You there, on the west end, lock your doors and keep the kiddies in. Be on the lookout." And sure enough, for the next few days, walking the two blocks to and from school, we saw many police cars. "Hurry along now"—they'd pull up alongside of us and roll down their windows—"get on home." Then the search shifted to the east side of town, to the railroad yards, and south toward the Ozarks.

Autumns in Missouri broke your heart. The tree-banked hill-sides turned brilliant reds and oranges against the wide green slopes. In the event of an early snow, the grass, arrested by the cold, might stay green all winter. The streets, sidewalks, drive-ways, lawns, even the river, took on a slow mosaic until every-thing was covered in leaves. It was ridiculous to rake them, though people did, and systematically burned them in the gut-ters in front of their houses. Saturdays, through October and November, the whole town smelled of burning leaves, though in the park across the road from us, we could still scoop oak, hickory, maple, and sycamore leaves into huge piles under which we'd bury one another, say prayers, and eulogize. The city cemetery lay to the west of us and we often watched the long processions of cars, headed up by the hearse, making their way to the gravesite. You were supposed to stop whatever you were doing and stand still while they passed. If we were in the car, our mother always pulled over. Our father said if people were about to die, they'd die in the autumn, and usually after midnight, when the body, he'd say, was just too tired.

During those days when the inmate was still at large, I can't say that we noticed a change in our mother. I must have been about eight that year. Connie was six, Eva, ten, and Gena was thirteen. David had just begun kindergarten, and he'd been a problem, that fall, for the rest of us at West School. He simply didn't want to go. "Once you stawt," he'd say, "you nevew stop." David had trouble with *r*'s. Some mornings he'd run out of the house in his pajamas and hide out in the orchard until we were all late. Then our mother would say "Never mind," and drive us to school in the car. "I'll be ready for him tomorrow," she'd reassure us. One morning David wrapped himself with his blanket around an apple tree. He held on tight, securing the end of the blanket in his teeth, and no one, not even our mother, could pry him loose. "Never mind," she said, grabbing the car keys. David stayed lashed to that tree even as we pulled out of the driveway.

Maybe Mother took those plates of food out to the fence in the evenings, after supper. Say she told us she was feeding the dogs or burning the trash. Or maybe she waited until we were all in school and had settled David, Beth, and Steve at the kitchen table where they drew or made maps and sculptures out of my mother's famous concoction of flour and salt and water. Whenever it was, it must have happened something like this. Our mother would round up our dogs, lure them into the garage with scraps, and close the door. That accomplished, she'd walk out toward the barn, probably no farther than the fence, call the inmate's name, set the food down, and wait. Near the barn, just beyond our hives, you could see a long way down the orchard slope, almost to the pond. She probably stood there awhile watching the sassafras bushes along the fence until she saw something stirring. By then the dogs had begun whining and barking. They wanted out or they'd mess on the concrete. Before she let them out, she'd retrieve the plate, which she claimed was always empty. "Poor thing," she'd say years later, when she finally told us the story.

The inmate was discovered by some neighbor children in our orchard about a week after he'd disappeared. They came on him asleep in a ditch near our pond and sneaked back up to their house to tell their mother, who called the police. When we came home from school that afternoon, three patrol cars sat in the driveway. The inmate sat in the one that had a grille, like the dogcatcher's truck, between the front and back seats. The famous gun lay in the front seat. We got a look at it. The judge had been called to identify the prisoner and he stood in his black overcoat chatting with the chief. The weather had turned cold that day. It happened like that, sometimes. A wind would come up and in a few hours, the temperature would drop thirty degrees. All of us stood shivering. We'd gone to school that morning in summer dresses. "Go in the house and get a sweater," our mother said, but we didn't want to miss anything. After a while the judge got into a squad car and was taken back to the courthouse. The neighbor children, having been thoroughly questioned, wandered on home. We watched them crossing our orchard like traitors. A policeman shut the door on the inmate. He was handcuffed and his prisoner's clothes were filthy. You could hardly see his face now, the autumn sky reflected in the glass. As he was driven off we stared at him and he at us. When we waved, he lifted his cuffed hands and smiled. He looked young, like one of our brothers, tired, and well fed.

CHAPTER 5 ORCHARD ACRES

The tracks above the pond hugged the hills to the east and west like warped ladders. When I learned the magic trick of drawing one point perspective, I often drew railroad tracks spreading through the center of some town whose buildings loomed larger and more detailed the closer they got to their creator. You could read the names of the streets and see in the window what the drugstore was selling, see the sidewalks cracked by the roots of trees. In the beginning I was no good at drawing people and left them out entirely. When I did try putting them in, crowds waiting to board, I was mostly dissatisfied and erased the ones close in, their profiles wrong, their eyes on the sides of their heads like birds, my omissions leaving pulpy smudges on the thick drawing pad. Then you could see how paper comes from wood. Once when my mother asked me why I had erased so many, I was a little hurt that she'd noticed. Then I told her that my picture showed the day after *the rapture*, and having said so, wrote at the bottom of the page, "One shall be taken, the other left," from the Book of Matthew.

Matthew's version of the Second Coming is an extreme

prophecy full of storms and angels sounding trumpets and the more delicate imagery of birds, fruit trees, the look of the sky in summer. And I believed that *the rapture* would happen, maybe in my lifetime. Certainly during the fifties nation was rising against nation. The networks broadcast the mushroom cloud over and over on "You Are There," and "Twentieth Century," those television shows airing on Sunday evenings after we'd spent nearly the whole day at church. Or if we drove for one reason or another to the interstate thirty miles northeast, we always passed through the tiny town of Kingdom City, where a huge billboard on which the tally to the minute of how many Missourians had been killed in car accidents warned us, PREPARE TO MEET YOUR MAKER. I was seven when the first Sputnik was launched and I connected it with Nikita Khrushchev's pounding his shoe on the table at the U.N. and shouting "We will bury you," this newsreel spliced between footage of various "famines, pestilences, and earthquakes in diverse places." Jesus might come back any day if that were the criterion.

And though we knew the "you" Jesus addressed in chapter 24 were his disciples, the pronoun directed out to us over the centuries was indicting, but also comforting, the way taking direction from a stranger once was to us comforting, and in the end, oddly exhilarating. Having set out on foot one June morning to investigate what were said to be bullet holes in the state prison's outer walls, Connie, David, and I became lost in Jefferson City's east end. As we sat along a curb trying to make sense out of David's toy compass, a man had come out of his house to help us. We stood up to listen, our full attention focused on the man's mouth as he routed us by signs and landmarks home. As he spoke our own lips moved as we tried to memorize the street names he offered, the gas station at McCarty and Main, the one with the winged horse, he said, over the pumps. Did we see our way now? We nodded. But he went over it one more time. He tousled David's hair as he did so. And all the way home we corrected and edited one another against the man's voice in our heads, remembering, with surprising affection, the lines around his mouth, the old teeth.

Maybe because we knew Matthew's version so well, we were suspect of others. Bored during the long sermons on Sunday mornings, Eva and I tried to tackle Revelation. But to Eva and me there was something wrongheaded about it. How, for example, we'd whisper angrily, could the end of the world be described in the past tense? "It's like telling someone your dream," our mother offered, delighted with our interest. Eva and I eyed each other. We hadn't been aware that our mother was listening. Then our mother left us to it. She'd look piously at the minister as if to say, "There are lessons going on as you speak."

But we had dreams. We had nightmares, which upon waking, we comforted each other into discounting. "It's just a dream." Eva would shake me awake. Until we were teenagers, Eva and I shared a bed. "Look," she'd say with practiced authority as she flicked on the bedside light. The objects in the room burned flat and innocuous. "Maybe you need to go to the bathroom," she'd suggest as she ran her hand under my legs, but it was usually too late. Eva would sigh and disappear into the bathroom to return with an armload of towels which we silently, ritualistically layered over the wet spot, climbed onto, and fell asleep.

In the morning I'd tell Eva my dream, though in the daylight the whole thing seemed foolish; the phantom who'd been chasing me, like an overdressed actor who didn't get the part slipping sheepishly into the wings. Besides, the plots of my dreams were predictable. For these reasons I often tried to spice up the beginnings. Instead of the usual "Someone was chasing me toward a ladder . . ." I'd offer something like "I gripped the loose rough rungs . . ." But Eva was on to me. She knew if she let me begin this way, the dream report would take a long time. Given license, I'd surely lie to make it interesting. Eva would stop what she was doing, braiding her hair or stripping the bed, and meet my eyes accusingly.

"Come off it," she'd insist. "Well, same old thing," I'd answer, disappointed. "The crooked house?" "Yes." "The guy in the big coat?" "Uh-huh." "Was that piano still up in the tree house?" "I think so." "Well, did you make it to the top of the ladder?" "No, I fell back, I was falling . . ." "Then how do you know about the piano?" Eva narrowed her eyes. No funny business, she seemed to be saying. "Look at it this way," Eva said once. She'd crossed the room to take me firmly by the shoulders. Even now, when Eva has some insight into my character, this is what she does. "If someone got a *piano* up there, for heaven's sake, you can make it too." Eva brought her foot back and kicked, stopping just short of my shin. "See? Then kick that devil in the face."

Some days I watched for *the rapture*, watched for it like changes in weather, mostly on summer afternoons when there was nothing else to do. And sure enough, once in a while, say late August, the air grew deathly still and the sky turned a yellowish green. The clouds on the horizon seemed actually to bubble. Blueing to black, they moved fast over the orchard, now and then leaking a funnel. Tornadoes were fairly common in Missouri, less so on our side of the river. People who'd survived them said they sounded at first like a freight train approaching, though they weren't as fast as you might think. For instance, you could outrun them in a car.

Tornadoes that hit the flatland on the other side of the river picked their way through the little towns there leaving some houses perfectly intact while devastating others, turning over boxcars, taking up dust, timber, appliances, trees, and more than a few people into clumsy whirlwinds that zigzagged for miles across open terrain before they dropped everything in a field and disappeared into the clouds. We were never hit directly because Jefferson City was spread out on the slopes behind the Missouri River bluffs, those hills continuing down through the Ozarks and into Arkansas. But the high winds in the tornadoes' wakes swept through the orchard now and then. They tore branches off trees and scattered the apples so far and wide we just let them rot in the weeds. And the birds went wild. They'd get drunk from eating the fermenting fruit and wheel and dive into windows or into the pond. It was awful to watch.

And sometimes those winds lifted the weather vanes off the tops of the house and the outbuildings. My father loved weather vanes. He'd mounted two on the house, a rooster, as I remember, and a whale. Now and then he'd climb three stories to the roof to clean or repair them. It was an activity which brought all of us from the kitchen or up from the pond since we knew it scared our mother. She always held the ladder for him and as he ascended she called out warnings. "Be careful," she'd begin reasonably, but the higher he got, the more shrill became her pleas. "We'll hire someone!" she'd shout as he reached the second-story gutters, as if the whole undertaking had been her own bad idea. "Come back down, Ev, now come on!" she'd sing as though she were coaxing a child from a closet, but she knew he wasn't listening. Now she barked instructions for us to get ready, for what we weren't sure. To watch. To catch him. And as if we might really be able to catch him we took positions at the corners of the house and by the back and front doors, trampling, as we scrambled, the yews that hid the wrought-iron staved fences around each window well.

The house, facing north, sat some distance from the street on a wide terrace, the orchard spreading out behind it. It was of Dutch Provincial design and we enjoyed that fact since we were what was called High Dutch. It was as if destiny had intended us to live there, as if our grandparents' journey from Holland during the nineteenth century, and then our parents' long trek inland in the early forties had all along had this destination, 2113 West Main Street. The house itself looked a little like a ship, its bricks painted white and the shutters on the many windows a marine blue. The blue tarpaper roof sloped down to meet the second-story eaves and pitched high above the front door. It was a big house, cluttered in back with additions and gabled windows, blue- and white-striped aluminum awnings, and a tiny balcony off the girls' suite over the back door, the whole surrounded by shrubs and flower gardens that grew tulips and daffodils in the spring, roses in summer, mums and marigolds in the fall. Some years, in February, impatient for the first blossoming, our mother stuck plastic crocuses in the stone planters.

Our parents had bought the house from its original owner, a Mr. Weber, though they knew the property pretty well already. Having moved from Columbia to Jeff City in 1947, they came often to buy apples. As the story goes, Weber took a liking to them, and when my mother became pregnant with her sixth child and it was clear they'd have to move into a bigger house, Weber offered them the property for a reasonable sum. I was the first child born there, the first to be brought home from St.

Mary's to Orchard Acres, as the grounds were called, and my father had a brass sign made that year of six children under an apple tree. He hung it from a lamppost at the bottom of the driveway. The fact that I was the first to be born in the house has given me a sense of ownership of the seasons there. And until I was ten, we mistakenly celebrated my birthday on February 2 instead of on February 6, the true day I was born.

That my parents associated my arrival with the story of the groundhog, who, as legend has it, predicts the onset of spring by whether he sees his shadow, only confirmed my feelings of ownership. I was disappointed the evening my mother stopped cutting my cake and looked quizzically at the ceiling, then dashed upstairs to the study to dig out my birth certificate. "I thought so," she sang as she returned to the table. She waved the document around. "All of a sudden I had this funny feeling . . . see, honey?" She came over to me and put her arm around my shoulder. I looked hard at the certificate, at the tiny heel print like an eclipsed moon. "Never mind"—my mother slipped it in her apron pocket and went back to the cake. "Listen," she said as she passed me a huge piece. "It's *your* birthday. *You* choose which day you'd like to celebrate from now on." So that in the years to follow, sometimes I chose the second, sometimes the sixth. And on Groundhog Day my mother never failed to ask me, "Well? Can you see your shadow?" "No," I'd answer because I knew how she loved an early spring. "Good!" she'd say. "Today I'll stop by Woolworth's and pick up some crocuses."

One August day my father went up his aluminum ladder. A storm the night before had lifted his weather vanes out of their sockets and strewn their parts across the lawn. To have his hands free he'd lashed the spoke crosses to his back, the rooster and the whale bobbing like a full quiver behind him. It must have

41

been one of those hazy summer days when after the rains everything gave off a protein breath. The tree toads clicked out long
dithyrambs and the jays, probably because their full nests had
been scattered, whined and swooped at the tree line. "Watch
it, Ev!" my mother, her feet planted on either side of the ladder,
called up to him. The sky was more white than blue. "Careful!"
she shouted as he reached the peak. Then she called to us to
take our places.

We heard the ladder bang against the side of the house as
our father left the top rung, heard his rubber boots digging into
the grit as he catwalked the peak. Then we heard a scraping,
sliding sound, like snow during a thaw when it suddenly gives
and tumbles. Did we cover our heads with our hands? Did we
extend our arms, as our mother had shown us, to break his
fall? The weather vanes clattered down the slope, sailed from
the roof, and hit the concrete. We heard a moan as the gutter
above the kitchen fell, barely missing David, and then "Dadblast
it!" our father called out, but he hung on, inching himself,
spread-eagled, back up the pitch. He lay as if pinned to the roof
a moment. He didn't speak again until he'd reached the spine.
Then he hoisted himself up with great effort to mount, like a
rider, the house.

Years later, during a brief stay in Holland, Michigan, I came
across an old Dutch saying on a plaque which you were to
hang, I suppose, in your kitchen. It translated, "Love your home
but don't ride the house." I laughed cynically. I was eighteen
and unhappy and sorry to be who I was. Sure, I thought. Heaven
forbid that the Dutch would ever love anything too much, ever
lose themselves, ever sin by loving. I stood in the souvenir shop
among the wooden shoes and china windmills and cursed the
ancestors. I missed the irony, the memory of my father strad-
dling the high blue peak of our house above the thousand trees

while the ten of us cheered him, while we rushed around on the ground collecting the four winds that had fallen from his back. "Bring 'em up to me, Paul!" he boomed when he'd secured his position. His hands and face were raw and bleeding. He'd lost his glasses and squinted in the glare. "Absolutely not, Everett Sugarbaker!" our mother shouted. "You come down this minute!" "Good night nurse, Ginny! Help Paul up!" and Paul started up the ladder. Never in our lives did we hear our father swear.

CHAPTER 6 *CLOTHO, LACHESIS, AND ATROPOS*

My mother called them the apparitions. She didn't mean it unkindly. It was like a name she'd given to figures in a dream that frightened her. My mother remembered her dreams. She didn't sleep well from years of having to get up to nurse or from our waking her to tell her our dreams. She rested on her side on the edge of a high antique bed, a hand across her forehead, as if she were trying to see against a light, rested like ancient tribesmen who lay down each night on the mounds of their ancestors to keep their own souls in place. Sometimes in the mornings we'd hear her telling a dream to our father. It was usually a disaster dream about one of our brothers who had already left home. She could see Everett in the distance. She waved but Everett did not wave back. Or Paul was calling to her and she could not answer. "Phone him this morning," our father would say, as if he believed her dream had been prophetic. The name, the apparitions, came from a dark place in her, like her mothering.

She was referring to a family, a woman and her two grown daughters, who lived across the field from us before the convent was built. A farmer had grown winter wheat there. Some years it was pasture where cattle grazed. Beyond the field to the south was a rendering facility which our dogs frequented. They'd drag up huge tendoned bones and lie like lions on the front lawn and chew with great animal concentration. You could not get the bones away from them. For years we nursed the idea that they'd brought down a steer. Before the convent our house lay nearly on the outskirts of Jefferson City's west end. The women's shack lay a little farther west on the opposite edge of the field backed by woods.

The women had no occupation that we knew of. Every six months or so they'd come to our house for handouts. We'd spot them walking along the street, turning up our driveway. Other times they'd cut through the field to the back door. They'd come for canned goods and clothing which our mother always seemed to have ready for them in boxes in the garage. Depending on the season, she might also offer them a bushel of apples and a few jars of honey. The clothing which she had folded in the boxes was hers. The daughters must have been in their twenties, though they had an ageless aspect. All three were big-boned and stocky with hair to their waists. The only distinction, it seemed, between the mother and her daughters was that her hair was iron gray while the daughters' was black.

They smelled bad and we said so to one another in whispers behind our mother, we who avoided baths whenever possible and let our hair, Sunday to Saturday, grow into a tangle, not bothering to pick out the sticktights. We dreaded the washing and the combing out. When she overheard our whispering, Mother shushed us and we were scolded later. "They're alone," she'd say, meaning they had no man. Each time they came by our mother invited them in and each time they declined, gathered their goods and set out again. Sometimes they'd pause among the trees on their way home and hold up to one another our mother's dresses, robes, or nightgowns—most were maternity clothes—leaving a few items hanging on a bough, maybe the items they didn't like, or maybe they simply forgot them.

Once under a hedge among the dogs' stash of bones we found a little New Testament which our mother had slipped into the women's box of canned goods. It had been through a rain or two so that the pages were swollen and yellow. This distressed our mother—not the fact of the ruined book, since we got them by the gross, free, from the Southern Baptist Convention Headquarters. Mother taught several Bible classes in Jefferson City and surrounding areas. The New Testaments were the Southern Baptists' contribution. The imitation-leather-bound books were all over our house. We raided each new shipment, claiming ours had been lost, though in fact we hoarded them. But our mother was worried by the find, by what she reasoned to be the women's indifference. "They can't be reached," she said as she tried to flatten out the hapless pages. For a moment she looked frightened. The apparitions were beyond religion, beyond any institution of the family as we knew it. "They're alone," she repeated, and slipped the little book in her apron pocket.

CHAPTER 7 THE DAUGHTERS
OF HANNAH

On Sunday afternoons our mother drove about
fifteen miles southwest to teach a Bible class at the women's
prison in Tipton. I'm not sure how many times we made that
trip or how many of us went along week to week. What follows
is more a story than a record. One particular Mother's Day
Sunday in the year, say, 1959, we dressed up for the occasion,
Eva, Connie, and I. By then Rena and Gena were in their teens
and maybe they didn't care to go along. Or maybe they needed
to stay home to look after our father, little Beth, and the two
youngest boys.

We stocked the back of the station wagon with bushel baskets
full of flowers, red and yellow roses from our arbors, and lilacs,
and maybe purple and yellow irises that grew so prolifically in
May. That day we also loaded two cake boxes full of red and
white carnations, which must have been donated by the local
florist, in order that the inmates could make for themselves
Mother's Day corsages. By the time we pulled out of the driveway the scent of flowers inside the car was nearly overwhelm-
ing. We drove with all the windows down through the May

fields toward Tipton, our hair blowing wildly as we leaned over the backseat and badgered our mother about the nature of the inmates' crimes.

"What did they do?" we shouted over the wind, "and why are they there?" "It doesn't matter!" our mother called back to us. "Their names are written in the Book of Life now!" But we knew that the only woman ever to be executed in the state of Missouri had been incarcerated for a time in Tipton. She'd been part of a famous kidnapping in which the child held for ransom had been killed. The story went that her husband had actually murdered the child but she'd confessed that she had stood by; she had not tried to stop him. After the couple's conviction, rumor had it that the prosecutor had given her a choice: life imprisonment or the gas chamber, and she had chosen the latter. The idea that a woman had been involved in the murder of a child was foreign to us, and horrifying. We wanted to talk about it. We wanted to figure it out. Our mother tried to distract us as she drove, telling us the story of the good thief on the cross or the story of Saul, a murderer of Christians, who was struck blind on the road to Damascus and converted on the spot. God even changed his name, she told us, to Paul.

But we would not be distracted. In our experience women were, without exception, young or old, rich or poor, given in one way or another to the care and nurturing of children. They were wives and mothers or widows with grown children or grandmothers or what our father called maiden ladies, who were our school and Sunday-school teachers. Even the nuns figured in our strictly maternal perceptions. Once, when our sister Rena had been hit by a car as she stepped out from behind the city bus—it was said that her violin case, which she'd held up broadside, had saved her life—hadn't the Sisters of St. Mary's sent a hand-painted sympathy card that read, in beautiful calligraphy: "For Rena Ann's full recovery. To this end our prayers are offered"?

Maybe there was one exception, a woman—a phantom really, since none of us had ever actually seen her—named Edna Knight. She was rumored to live in the Pacific Hotel across the street from the train station. Eva, who would have been twelve that year, claimed Edna Knight was a prostitute, though she did not use that word. Rather, Eva described her as "a lady who does, you know, things for men for money." We hadn't a clue as to what Eva meant. Still, we nodded. Eva had no doubt come across this information in Sunday school because our church sat on a hilltop above the depot. From the church's new wing called the Educational Building you could watch during the long lessons the trains coming and going and the barges making their slow progress upriver. And if the sun was right, not too high midmorning—in the winter or early spring—you could see down the hill into the broad storefront windows to the Pacific Hotel lobby wherein a handful of men, probably railroad workers—"Edna's friends," Eva called them—chalked their cues and stepped up to the pool tables. Above them, as Eva explained, behind one of the shuttered second-story windows, Edna Knight was said to do business.

The women's prison lay on the outskirts of the tiny town of Tipton. It was a series of sallow brick buildings on an expanse of dusty yards and dry gardens, the whole of it bordered by a chain-link fence. It looked different from the state prison for men, the latter surrounded by a stone wall topped with barbed wire, the guard houses positioned obviously at the four corners in which you could see men in uniform with guns. The prison for men was a much larger facility located in Jefferson City on an east bluff overlooking the river. It sat about three blocks from the First Baptist Church. During a prison riot in the fifties we'd heard gunshots as we sat in the sanctuary and we could smell smoke from the fires the inmates had set in the yard. We sang on. Some prisoners did escape during that particular riot. They were caught down by the tracks where they'd tried to hide out in the empty boxcars near the sandbars. It was said that several escapees were never seen again. Maybe they stole boats from the concrete plant and made their way at night downriver, or they drowned, since the currents by Jefferson City are deadly. Or maybe they made it to some town where they could hop a train west.

We arrived at the prison early so we'd have time to set up the classroom. A woman guard let us, car and all, past the booth at the main gate, her radio blaring as she popped her gum and smiled widely and waved us through. Someone opened a side door for us, into a sort of recreation building. It looked like a school with its institutional green walls, its polished linoleum floors and fluorescent lights. As we followed a guard down the hall we could see into a ceramics room, a sewing room, a tiny library. The first time I'd accompanied my mother to the Bible class I'd whispered to Eva that it hardly looked to me like a prison. "Look at the windows," she'd answered, and sure enough, behind the orange and brown fringed muslin curtains, all the windows were wire mesh. They could only be opened automatically, the panes sliding sideways inside their cages when the guard put a key in a fuse box at the back of the room.

The Bible classroom was on the ground floor, and on first appearance it too seemed ordinary. Many folding chairs were stacked against a wall. My sisters and I set them up in rows to face the desk at the front. On a freestanding blackboard next to a piano our mother wrote the verses that accompanied her lesson. Initially our mother played the piano for her Bible class, but she did not play, I'm afraid, very well. She usually hit the right keys but her timing was thrown off as she leaned up to read the music. She'd peer hard over her glasses, strike a chord, then look down at her fingers and sway forward to decipher the next bar. Sometimes she'd get lost and have to start over. It was so hard to follow her lead that mostly we mumbled the hymns. But one Sunday an inmate shyly approached Mother to say that she knew how to play. Might she try the opening hymn? "By all means!" our mother answered, but my sisters and I knew she was disappointed. "Blessed Be the Tie" was the only piece our mother practiced during the week. She'd nearly learned it by heart. As the inmate began, though, it was clear that she had a gift as she flourished the text with trills and double chords so that we went cleanly on to the second and third verses, after which the artist deftly changed keys and began "Jesus Saves," then "Great Is Thy Faithfulness." The piano bench creaked as she lifted her hands at the end of each hymn.

And so it was settled, and the woman—let's say her name was Betty Lynn—was allowed to come early each week to decide with our mother what hymns would be appropriate to the lesson. As they chatted, my sisters and I arranged the flowers in huge peanut butter and pickle jars which the guards had set, full of water, on either side of the desk. That Mother's Day Sunday we also opened the boxes full of carnations and set them on the desk along with a pile of rubber bands and sewing pins. As the women filed in—about thirty of them, each wearing a pale green uniform—they were directed to pass by the desk and choose flowers for their corsages.

It was a custom in the Midwest, maybe all over the world, its origins, as I understand it, Presbyterian, that on Mother's Day one wore a red flower if one's mother was alive and a white flower if she was dead. Our mother had complicated the custom for the occasion. She instructed the women, as they filed past, to choose, each one, flowers to reflect how many children they had. If, for instance, an inmate's mother was still living and she, the inmate, had three children, she was to make for herself a corsage of three red carnations, securing them at the stem with a rubber band. Then the woman could pin the corsage on her uniform or wear it around her wrist prom-fashion.

Maybe the instructions were muddled since the boxes were empty by the time the last group filed by. The guard frowned. "You don't have no six kids." She turned to an inmate sporting a huge red and white corsage. The woman looked behind her, as if the guard must surely be talking to someone else, then covered her flowers with her hands. "Give them back," ordered the guard. Her irritation included our mother, as if the guard found the corsage making silly to begin with, a sentimental complication which, just as she could have predicted, had led to trouble. "Never mind," our mother intervened without hesitation. She began picking the big blossoms off our arrangements of irises and roses. "This will do just fine, won't it, dear?" Mother pinned the flowers on the inmate next in line. The guard clicked her tongue and narrowed her eyes at the thief, as if the incident had a future. "And what about you?" Mother turned on the guard, who, startled, broke into a grin. "None for me, thank you, Mrs. Sugarbaker." But our mother moved quickly. "Oh, come on." She removed her own corsage of ten white carnations and pinned it to the guard's lapel.

By now Betty Lynn had begun playing the introductory chords to "Blessed Be the Tie," and my sisters and I passed the hymnals down the rows. We hadn't much time for singing that Sunday because of the corsage making. It was stuffy in the classroom and in a moment the guard put her key in the fuse box, the windows sliding sideways as the guard tapped her watch, signaling for our mother to begin. Mother stepped before the group and spoke. "What a blessing to us are our children. And how difficult it must be for all of you to be away from yours . . ." She touched the damp spot on her blouse where her corsage had been.

From where we sat in the back row my sisters and I could watch the audience without being noticed. A few of the women shed tears. Connie pinched me in alarm. "But let me tell you a story," our mother continued. "The Bible tells us about a woman named Hannah. Isn't that a pretty name? Hannah," she repeated. "Well, Hannah was one of two wives of a man named Elkanah . . ." Some of the inmates snickered. Connie seized my arm. Mother met the snickering with a grin. "I'm awful glad God changed that law, aren't you?

"Now . . ." Mother paced in front of the room as she spoke. "It so happened that the other wife—her name was Peninnah—had many sons and daughters. Our Hannah, poor thing, was barren. For some reason she simply couldn't have babies. We're told that 'God shut up her womb.' " Mother picked up some chalk and wrote the characters' names on the blackboard under her Scripture reference, 1 Samuel, chapters 1 and 2. A crescent of perspiration showed under the arms of her pale blue blouse. The smell of flowers in the room was sickening. "Of course this made Hannah unhappy. The Bible tells us that she even stopped eating—have you ever felt that sad?—she couldn't eat a thing!"

Our mother opened her own dog eared old Bible. A few photos fell out on the floor, a pressed flower, the envelope full of sand from Lake Michigan. She let them lie there as she read like an actress: "Then said Elkanah her husband to her, 'Hannah, why weepest thou? and why eatest thou not? and why is

53

thy heart grieved? am not I better to thee than ten sons?' "
Again the inmates snickered. Our mother pulled a lace hankie
from her belt and wiped her forehead and laughed too, exag-
gerating a sigh. "Men just don't understand these things, do
they?" She shook her head slowly for effect.

It was never clear to my sisters and me whether the inmates
were humoring our mother or laughing at her. Maybe they
thought her to be naive, or too theatrical, since now and then
we watched them elbow one another as she read or joked. Then
Eva would elbow me and nod toward the eye rollers as if to
mark them, as if to bear witness to their betrayal. But in the
next moment that pair would give our mother their full attention
so that we registered the impact of her words through their
expressions and turned, ourselves, back to her. "But
Hannah"—Mother was singing now—"would not be comforted. Hannah was in bitterness of soul, and prayed to the Lord
and wept sore!" "Amen!" returned an inmate. Was she making
fun? "Yes, Hannah prayed to God, ladies! She said, 'God, if
you'll give me a son—if you'll just let me have one little baby
boy—just one—I promise I'll give him to you. He'll be my gift
to you . . .'

"And you know what?" Mother quieted. She laid her Bible
on the desk and came close to the group. "God heard Hannah.
He heard her as he hears us all when we need him. And sure
enough, Hannah conceived." Mother beamed. "Can you imagine her joy? Can you imagine? Listen"—she tried to involve
the group—"how many of you have sons? Give me a show of
hands here." She raised her right hand as she counted, "One,
two, four, seven, eight, nine—keep them up—eleven, my good-
ness!" Eva and I suspected a hoax. Nearly all the women, grinning at one another, had raised their hands. Maybe it was a
way of justifying in front of the guard their huge corsages.

Mother blushed. Her eyes met the guard's. "Well, I suppose it's possible. I have four sons myself, and of course, my lovely girls . . . Girls, stand up a moment, will you? Come on now . . ." She smiled, an edge to her request. The three of us stood as the inmates turned to look at us.

"Thank you, darlings." She sighed. She seemed calmer now. "Yes, God heard his Hannah and she conceived and gave birth to her heart's desire, a little boy, and she named him Samuel." Mother underlined the name on the board. "See? She gave birth to a great man, as you may have—who's to say? *Two* books of the Bible are named for him. You know . . ." Our mother sat on the edge of the desk, Bible in hand. She was sweating profusely. Stained pink from her rouge, her hankie hung limp at her waist. "It's one thing, though, to promise someone something and another thing to keep a promise . . ." Some of the inmates slumped now in their chairs or fanned themselves with the hymnals or dozed in the heat. A few still listened wistfully. "Imagine it." Mother tried to illustrate. "Imagine Hannah holding her baby boy at last, rocking him, singing to him . . . and remembering her promise, too."

Mother looked tired, strangely younger. She backed up to the window and looked out at the sky. Maybe she did so for effect. Outside the window was the prison's modest playground, a slide, some swings. The inmates' children used them during visiting hours. "But a promise is a promise," she said. Anyone still listening guessed the conclusion: biblical, therefore unequivocal. It disappointed our mother to have to report it. "And so in time, the Bible tells us, after Samuel was weaned, Hannah brought him to the temple, and there he lived all through his boyhood and into manhood and he became a great prophet and a great leader . . ."

Beyond her, through the wire mesh, visitors had begun to

gather on the playground. You could hear the swings creaking, a child's shriek, men's low voices. The women shifted in their chairs. "Like Hannah," our mother tried to begin again, "we all make sacrifices." It was as if she'd intended this part to be the core of her lesson but she'd arrived at it too late. The guard tapped her watch. "Like Hannah," our mother pleaded, "we've had to give our children up for a time." The inmates arranged their hair or eyed Mother impatiently. Some turned in their chairs to look at us. She tried to qualify. "I don't mean we—I mean you—I— Listen." She gave up. "No one understands this better than you. It is a special knowledge. I wouldn't know what it's like. But I'm praying for you," she said. "I pray for you every day. Would you pray for me too?" Mother sat down on the piano bench and smoothed her skirt over her legs.

CHAPTER 8 THE BUILDERS

A tragedy occurred in the orchard in the spring of 1962. A neighbor child wandered down to the pond alone one evening and drowned. Whether she'd tried to swim or catch a frog or dragonfly, no one would ever know. She was found the morning following her disappearance. There was a small funeral which I remember my mother attending. Later, over the phone, I heard my father offering to have the pond filled in. More and more it was the case that we encountered strangers in the orchard, mostly children, who found their way from the new subdivisions that went up in the late fifties. The subdivisions had been built to accommodate the workers at the various factories erected to the south of us beyond the tracks, off a recently paved road called Industrial Drive.

One group of children I remember particularly since their family, like us, had many children. It was hard to distinguish one child from another because their hair had been cropped short above their ears—boys and girls alike—and the family resemblance was strong. They all looked to be under the age of eight or nine with several sets of twins between them, and we played with them sometimes, but as children do, without exchanging names. For the most part they seemed to want to keep to themselves and we caught sight of them in the early mornings out beyond the fence, where they squatted around some special flower or dead animal. They wouldn't wave if you called to them.

They were without shoes or coats, even in the winter, and the two smallest wore only T-shirts and urine-soaked underwear, so that my mother took to rounding them up by the back door. When they'd congregated silently around her, she'd slip their little goose-pimpled arms into our jackets and, bending over so that her nightgown showed under her overcoat, she lifted their feet into pairs of elastic-waisted corduroys and double knotted the Buster Browns she saved in the basement. Several times we found the clothes stacked neatly on the back steps, and my mother suspected that their mother had been offended and returned them. Then we simply kept the clothes in a bushel basket outside the kitchen under an awning and it would empty or fill, depending on the weather.

Nineteen sixty-two was a bad year. For the first time I took the bus with Eva to the junior high school, and because it was some distance from us, we had to rise early and leave the house in the fall and winter before it was light. We were tired when we arrived at the huge soot-red brick building that stood atop a steep, bald hill on the east end of town. After school we'd walk the half mile or so to our father's clinic and wait for him in the hall while he finished with the last of his patients. It was his habit to leave the bad news until the end of the day. When he discovered that one of his patients was dying of cancer and the operation had not helped, or worse, no operation was possible, he'd make an appointment with that patient and his or her family at around three in the afternoon. Then he'd usher them past us into his office. Sometimes we'd hear weeping or angry voices or pleading, followed by our father's condolences and advice. As I remember he'd often say that the best thing about cancer was that it allowed you time to make arrangements for the family, spend time with loved ones. On those particular afternoons the three of us rode home in silence and the houses along High Street looked trapped in time, as if years had passed since we'd seen them, and it was dark when we set foot in the kitchen. As a result we rarely went out into the orchard and began to notice its changes less and less, or maybe we were upset by its changes and so avoided it.

Now, instead of woods, we were bordered on two sides by treeless subdivisions. Now if you sat on the gate to the entrance you saw, beyond our tangled hillside, a huge corrugated factory with its vast parking lots, and beyond it, the new cloverleaf. You could not help but hear the traffic above the birds and the whine and grind of factory machinery that would intensify, then cease, as if something at that moment had been sheared off. And now came the contractors up the driveway. They'd offer my father a fair price for the orchard, to which he'd shake his head and walk out of the room. Sometimes they'd follow him to the foot of the stairs, or turn on my mother and in their bantering they made the orchard seem like a sentimental indulgence.

And maybe during that particular time some would say they were justified. What could the orchard matter in light of world and local news? In light of missiles pointed straight at us or the race riots or the dead president or the war whose soldiers came, more and more each day, from Jefferson City? Couldn't our father let it go or let part of it go? What could it mean to him or his family or the drowned girl or later her father, who was found facedown, drunk, drowned too in a foot of pond water?

Fear is subtle in the way that it confuses the present with the past and the future. So it obscures the moment, the hour, the season, each passing so painfully, everything becomes a candidate for fear's body. My father didn't sell the orchard. Instead, on the raised lawn outside the back door where many apple trees stood among flower gardens and arbors on which climbed, each spring, wild yellow roses, construction began on a fallout shelter. Bulldozers drove up one day and leveled the trees and the gardens, leaving huge tread marks in their wake, and dug a pit twenty feet by twenty feet and squared it off. *And the angel poured out his vial upon the rivers and they became like blood . . .* So a well was dug in the center of the pit and water gushed high into the air one April day. *And men were scorched with fire . . .* So the walls and the floors and the ceiling were reinforced with steel and concrete and lead panels one foot thick. And twelve stairs led down to the door. And inside, by a fluorescent light powered by an emergency generator you could see the shower and the toilet at the center of the one big room and twelve beds that, unhinged, flew down from the walls, and the shelves stacked with canned and dry goods and apple preserves and honey. And then the whole thing was covered over with dirt and sodded and it looked like a new grave. But it wasn't a grave, nor had it a grave's integrity.

That same year someone began clearing the field next to us. The oaks and the sassafras and maples were cut down and their stumps unearthed and carted away. Everything came up or was ground under. In a few days' time you could walk to the property line as though to the edge of a water and look out over many acres of earth into which, after a rain, you'd sink to your ankles. The stones we threw were swallowed, and one afternoon

I lost my mother's watch when it slipped from my wrist as I tiptoed on the maze of planks the crews had thrown down across the quagmire. Though we searched and searched, taking off our shoes and socks and feeling through the cold mud with our toes like vineyarders, we never found it.

The purpose of the excavation was a mystery to us until one night at the dinner table our father announced that the Catholic Church had purchased and cleared the land. Jefferson City possessed a large Catholic population. There were two Catholic churches downtown and several parochial schools, and our father practiced at a Catholic hospital. Its staff consisted mainly of nuns, from the administrator to the cooks. Some of the doctors and most of the nurses were nuns who wore starched white habits. Among the beads and crucifixes around their necks and waists, they wore also the serpent and the sword. Though we had friends from the Catholic schools who swore the nuns were a mean breed, strict beyond reason and unjust in the classroom, our relationship to them was different, maybe because we were outsiders.

When my father took us on rounds, for instance, the nuns, bending the rules, would sneak us up to see the newborns. My mother had seven of her ten children at St. Mary's, and though we were not Catholic, she said she had allowed each of us, at the nuns' request, to be sprinkled upon our arrival with water from the River Jordan. I remember those little vials from a time when Rena, following an accident, spent some time in the hospital. After one of our visits, Connie took me aside and, opening her palm, showed me happily that she'd stolen one from the dresser. It was a pretty little bottle with a cut glass stopper which we used, after dumping out the water, for our Evening in Paris cologne.

.   .   .

61

I have no recollection of the births of Connie, David, and Beth, but the birth of my youngest brother and the circumstances that surrounded it I remember vividly. My father had taken us with him when the hospital had called to say our mother's labor was advancing, and since he was a doctor at St. Mary's he pulled the station wagon up to the emergency entrance and went up alone, leaving us to play among the statues in the March-brown gardens and push one another around in the wheelchairs we found at the entrance. We dared one another to be lowered down into the window wells along the hospital's walls that looked in on the basement because we knew for a fact the morgue was located inside.

We played for several hours and then it began to get dark and my older sisters began to worry that our mother's labor was taking too long, as, indeed it was. She'd gone in early that morning and this was, after all, her tenth child. Upon hearing this, we younger ones began to cry. Soon we were all crying and so we locked ourselves in the car and cried and sang until we fell asleep. We were awakened near two in the morning as our father, looking grim and exhausted, opened the car door. He didn't speak all the way home, and my mother and Stephen, whose name means "crowned," and for whom my younger son is named, didn't come home for a long time.

After the excavation and the April rains, the earth dried a red-brown and huge cracks ran its shadowless length. We could play a game of baseball there, but mostly we complained about the loss of the wheat field in which we'd played hide-and-seek and looked for arrowheads, and where we'd teased the bulls that grazed there and that chased us, to our delight, up into the border trees. The row of sassafras, to which we'd escorted friends, torn off twigs, and made them chew, were gone, and the oak that had held a tree house. For us to try to imagine a building where there had been pasture was like trying to imagine summer in the dead middle of winter. We'd look at the apple trees shadowed in snow like the negative of a photograph and though someone might say, "These branches will soon be covered with leaves—you'll go barefoot—you'll dig with the dogs for a cool place under the hedges—" we couldn't believe it. We watched the sky, especially in the evenings when the clouds to the west sometimes opened a little and we could glimpse suddenly their long perspective, like ships off a tropical shoreline. Still, they were a long way off. In this way the field lay oppressive and foreign to us most of the spring. Then, in May, gravel was thrown down for the vehicles and the foundation for the convent was laid.

It went up quickly. Inside of a few weeks we could see from our upstairs windows how a huge rectangular structure would look out on something like a courtyard, and when the workmen left each day, we were all over it, the echoes from their buzz saws and hammers still ringing in our ears. We collected the wood scraps with which we'd make boats for David and Stevie to float on the pond, or "radios," which were nothing more than blocks riveted with nails and strung, then, with the colorful electrical wire we found. When the real wiring began, we picked the plugged nickels out of the sawdust and the younger ones fought over them like money.

It was best those warm spring evenings to climb to the second story with my sisters and walk the halls still without a roof or walls. It was a little like walking the deck of a ship moored in calm waters. You could see a long way from there, see over the hundreds of budding apple trees and over the fallout shelter's bright new sod dotted for the first time with dandelions, like lights among the smaller yellow rashes of chickweed, see where the orchard dropped away to the pond. You were just high enough, or maybe low enough, that the orchard looked immense and serious against the sharp spring sky. We learned that the convent would be home to a group of young Irish nuns not much older than we were, nuns who pledged never to leave there, or speak, except on special occasions like Christmas and Easter, and so we were pleased to notice how the tiny bedrooms on the convent's east side looked out over the orchard to the broad west side of our house where our own bedrooms were.

As we strolled through those rooms speculating and arguing and deciding or slipped like phantoms through the laths or sat down to play a game of jacks on the smooth sun-warmed plywood, it was as if we were blessing the convent by giving it a little history, as if the wood could retain our voices, or after the walls were paneled and the roof secured, our laughter. One afternoon we discovered a high swivel chair on the second story, probably a barber chair, our mother told us later; the nuns must keep their hair short under their habit. We spun one another around faster and faster, our own long braids whipping across our faces. Another day we found a series of glass-eyed statues of the saints in the courtyard which Connie and Beth hugged and talked to, and, struggling with their weight, dragged them through the dust and arranged them in a line, smallest to tallest.

By now our oldest sister, Rena, had left home along with our two oldest brothers, Everett and Paul. Gena was seventeen that May. Eva was fifteen and I had just turned thirteen. Connie was eleven, and so on down the line, every two years or so, David, Beth, and Stevie. Most of our names came from the Bible—you could open our mother's King James and find yours underlined in the text, and next to it the date of your birth—or we were named for our parents and grandparents or for our mother's favorite heroines. Eva's true name is Evangeline. We had Faith, Hope, and Charity in our midst in the form of my sisters' middle names. This was the spring of 1963 when we played every day until dark in the half-built convent.

One afternoon in late June we found the doors padlocked and the windows on the first story wired shut. Not long after that a six-foot wall went up and then the building too was bricked and we never went in again, though for a few more years we'd stay up late on Christmas Eve to watch from our bedroom windows the procession of shadows carrying candles in the windows across the trees. And once, when I was in trouble, I ran from the house and hid in the tiny chapel near the convent's entrance. I lay down on one of the pews, and as I listened to the nuns singing vespers behind a black curtain, I fell asleep. And one day in the spring of her graduation, my sister Eva and I took a walk along the wall. Just for fun we hoisted each other up and peeked over. It was beautiful in there. Everything had been sodded or seeded and there were lilac and azalea bushes blooming and roses climbing trellises, like those that completely obscured, now, the fallout shelter's entrance. Across the huge green lawn a clothesline had been strung and many muslin gowns hung drying, maybe nightgowns, and they were lifting like sails, almost in unison, in the breeze and the spring sunlight.

CHAPTER *9* HOME ECONOMICS

I used to envy the girls who excelled in Home Economics. They possessed a peace, I thought, a certainty, and when, in the mandatory eighth-grade class, I was assigned to a cooking foursome, I felt as shy around them as I did around my friends' mothers. The other three girls looked to be experts. They wore dresses they'd made themselves of some tiny floral design on which they'd hand-stitched perfectly centered lace collars and set them off with novelty buttons, red hearts down the bodice or anchors or daisies they'd bought in the notions aisle at Woolworth's. In this way they seemed above fashion, at the same time fresher and older than I. Their hair, bobbed short, they pulled simply to the side with barrettes and did not shave their legs.

What a sanctuary was the Home Economics suite in the middle of the three-story, drafty junior high that schooled all of Jefferson City's Protestant seventh, eighth, and ninth grades, along with students bussed in from Holt's Summit, Cedar City, Brazito, and other rural communities. One room hummed with about fifteen sewing machines, the finest work, say, a spring

66

ensemble, including a hand-stitched and blocked matching pink pillbox hat, carefully pinned in shop window fashion on a bulletin board and framed with cutouts from the Simplicity or Butterick or the rather avant-garde Mary Quant catalogs. The floor was always littered with fabric and colorful trim. At the end of the day our teacher, Mrs. Harris, swept everything up in a pile and we were allowed to stop by and sort through it if we wanted. Many of the mothers were quilters or we had little sisters who'd make doll clothes from the remnants.

Next to the sewing room was the cooking lab, five partitioned kitchens, each with its own sink and stove and refrigerator and a wide scrubbed counter on which sat, depending on the season, violets in perfume bottles or Queen Anne's lace in bright jars of food coloring or tea roses in cafeteria drinking glasses. And though we cringed at the smell of the creamed eggs or the beef Stroganoff we'd prepared and were supposed to eat in the remaining fifteen minutes before heading off to gym class (a whole meal, complete with appetizer—V-8 juice—and dessert—a soupy fruit Jell-O) we sat down proud of our accomplishments. Those miniature kitchens radiated a planetary warmth. Autumn or spring, east light flooded the room whose institutional windows were softened by dotted Swiss curtains. You could make out the outline of the bluffs and beyond the bluffs, there was the river, bordered on our side by the tracks.

We said grace over the food in spite of the recent Supreme Court decision to ban prayer in schools—it didn't seem to apply to us in Missouri—and sat for a while, elbows off the table, then scraped the plates and washed the dishes to the ten a.m. train sounding its arrival, and soon after, its departure, as though we were already women comfortable with waiting, first to marry, and once married, waiting to conceive a child, then another, the man, whoever he was, a shape in the doorway, someone boarding a train or, in the dusty distance, pulling a combine through a field. Everything we read or watched on TV in the fifties and sixties said it would be so. Even the textbooks, save the sciences, illustrated a future in which we would be women in dresses surrounded by children, the man alongside of us wearing a uniform or an overcoat and hat, the brim obscuring his features.

I tried to be like the experts, to succeed in Home Economics. I took new care with my appearance, cut my hair and bought poodle barrettes and anklets with flowers on the cuffs. From the Home Economics library I checked out *The Seventeen Guide to Etiquette* and studied closely the models in their white gloves and hats—usually small affairs with tiered veils—and their tailored walking suits and party dresses. Where were they going? It didn't matter. From my sisters' fashion magazines I cut out the pieces called "Make Me Over," and taped them to Eva's and my bureau mirror. On the left side I lined up the series of photographs of girls who stared glumly at the camera, their too-long bangs accentuating, said the caption, their big noses, or their over-permed hair a flat fuzz hugging their cheeks.

But on the right side of the mirror, after several months' regimen of face scrubs and creams, after a "good cut" by professionals and a fashion consultation that took into account their flaws, their "full-figured hips" or "Victorian busts," they were changed, perfectly ordinary, happy teens. They looked confident now, smiling. And now they were doing things, cutting out a dress in a light-flooded room or posing for a dive in a skirted one-piece bathing suit above a blue, blue pool. "I feel so feminine," said one caption under a picture of a blonde in a pink angora sweater. She held a kitten. "I want to be a fashion consultant," said another, "and I plan to major in textile design."

To succeed in Home Economics required more, however, than changing one's appearance. There were tests to be passed, first in the cooking then the sewing segment. In the former we were, among other tasks, to memorize the precise contents of the utensil drawers, exactly alike in each miniature kitchen. They were to be perfectly kept, soup and dessert spoons, salad and dinner forks laid one on top of another, the knives in measured rows with their blades facing to the right. The cooking drawer held, in sequence, the egg beater, ladles, the potato masher, along with wooden spoons, cake and pie servers, and serving forks. Below, another drawer held various mixing bowls, baking tins, colanders. Mrs. Harris, a small, immaculate woman with graying red hair, who wore walking suits and white gloves and various hats to school, even drew diagrams of each drawer on mimeograph paper that we could study at home. Many of the girls sighed with relief as Mrs. Harris passed out her diagrams, and she nodded with sympathy and approval. Not much was known about Mrs. Harris. Rumor had it that her husband was disabled. This was why, we gossiped, she had to work. There was an air of sacrifice about her which we confused with her waft of feminine smells, her lavender perfume, her minty breath.

Once it had been a terrible thing to have gotten breasts. No more slipping easily under fences, no more hard embraces shinnying up a tree, nor could I any longer, said my mother, strip to the waist evenings with my brothers to chase our gone-wild-in-the-orchard horse, corner her, bridle her, and tie her up so we could ride her the next day. As for playing sumo wrestlers with David after our baths, wrapping white towels around our waists and slicking our torsos with baby oil, of course that was out, too. It was as if such small physical alteration had meant sudden, irrevocable commitment to a sex I hadn't had time to consider yet. Hadn't my parents said it all along? I'd weighed eleven pounds at birth. They'd been sure I was a boy. They'd repeat this fact as though I'd duped them as I carved out another Boy Scout derby or dribbled in for a lay-up. But it pleased me to know I baffled them. It set me apart from the others. And secretly, I urinated standing up. When I heard the rock and roll songs on the radio I sang with cynicism and authority only the men's parts, "Come along and be my party doll," and "Let me be your candy man." My brothers had taught me to shoot the .22, and by the age of eleven I'd become a pretty good shot.

My sisters, too, marveled at and mothered me. As a result, I got away with things—not having to do the dishes, for instance, or to stay in on Saturday mornings to do housework. "I'm going hunting," I'd apologize to Rena as I rolled on a second pair of socks. "*She's* going *hunting*," Rena would repeat to Gena and roll her eyes. In these situations my sisters always talked about me in the third person. "Let her go," Gena would answer like a lenient parent. Then, as my breasts came, my family was no longer baffled. The restrictions and responsibilities that applied to my sisters now applied to me. I was a girl for sure, limited to it, like discovering my exoskeleton.

But in the classrooms of Home Economics that fall I began to believe I'd discovered a context nearly as subversive. For there we were in the middle of the morning cooking, of all things, sewing, and more than these, plotting our futures, naming our children after our favorite movie stars, while around us the school buzzed with purpose. Outside, the city went on with its industries. Men made laws in the capitol or dredged the river or lined up at the recruiting centers or were hired in the world or fired in the world. As for us, we were laughing, brushing one another's hair or blotting deftly borrowed lipstick before entering, like conspirators, the hallways. There was freedom in this not unlike the times Eva and I had dared to skip Sunday school to walk the empty streets downtown to the bus depot where, ordering black coffee at the counter, we assumed the pose of women waiting, perching ourselves demurely on the swivel stools as we perfected the art of peering into our huge purses. Whom or what did we practice to be waiting for? "Him," we'd say flatly to one another, inventing the script as we went along. We didn't dare giggle. The point was to convince others that we were, in fact, waiting as women wait so profoundly as to become invisible, and free.

Each time I took the Home Economics test I failed it, though I'd studied long and hard. When given the three blank sheets of paper on which I was to re-create Mrs. Harris's drawings, all I could see were my mother's drawers where utensils, pencils given to us by our milkman Henry, Popsicle sticks, toys from the Cracker Jack boxes, a few screwdrivers, etc. were thrown in together. My mother's drawers, kitchen or otherwise, made heroes and heroines of us all at one time or another, as much for what they were missing as for what they contained. If we were to find something just when our parents needed it, for instance, at dinnertime, the potato masher, a little rusty from a week in the sandbox, or, as my father worked on the tractor, the Phillips head screwdriver—to this day in my experience a rare and exotic object—we were much celebrated. "You found it!" my mother would sing as I held up the masher. She shook her arm and smiled to show me how I'd saved her the aching task of hand whipping the Idahos. "Debbie found it!" my brothers and sisters shouted, calling off the search, their voices tinged with envy as my father entered the back door. "Good for you, Deb," he'd greet me and tousle my hair. "She always had eagle eyes." He'd wink at my mother in passing. "And such a marvelous memory," my mother'd confirm. She dropped her voice on the last word to exaggerate, for my benefit, a note of wistful awe. And surely that evening, and if it was a vital find—the tractor jack among the baseball bats, or my mother's glasses among the Ball dome lids—into the next day, the hero or heroine would be treated specially. He or she would certainly be offered the gizzard at Sunday dinner.

How was it, then, that I was to render on paper drawers that precluded any possibility of loss, of celebrity? And what dull drawers they'd be without seed packs, emery boards, flashlights oozing battery acid, party favors, hairbrushes, test tubes, toothpicks, a little music box in the shape of a piano full of Bible verses that played, no matter how many times you dropped it, "Standing on the Promises." Sentenced day after day to afterschool detention where I'd be presented with three blank sheets of paper, I sat among a handful of other failures, smart-mouthed girls, most of them older than I, who'd flunked whole grades and who were simply "doing time," they'd tell me, until their sixteenth birthday, when they could quit school for good, girls sent home nearly every day for wearing stretch pants to class or miniskirts, girls who smoked in the bathrooms and teased their hair so high you could make out the domes of their skulls in the light-filled library.

In Jefferson City such girls and their male counterparts were called Hoods. It was rumored that they were capable of great cruelty. All were seasoned shoplifters and proudly wore the earrings or makeup they'd lifted from the Woolworth's counter. After the summer sidewalk sales called Dog Days, they flaunted skirts, sweaters, scarves, jackets, even shoes. This was their second, and for some, their third year in Home Economics, and they jeered Mrs. Harris each time she'd leave the room and cross the hall to her suite to look in on the experts. Some voluntarily stayed after school to buttonhole a blouse or try a soufflé. Mrs. Harris let them listen, after hours, to the Easy Days music station on the radio while they worked, and each time she opened her door we in detention heard some scrap of "Harbor Lights," or "The Sunny Side of the Street." The high library windows were brilliant, those afternoons, with autumn foliage, the maples like huge yellow lampshades on the hillsides. The blank pages before me swarmed with leaf shadows.

"Then shall the kingdom of heaven," I read in my Bible one night following detention, "be likened unto ten virgins, which took their lamps, and went forth to meet the bridegroom. And five of them," it said, "were wise and five were foolish. They that were foolish took their lamps and took no oil with them . . ." Reading my Bible each night was a habit I'd cultivated after my conversion the previous year. I'd been twelve and had "gone forward." In our Baptist Church, going forward meant hearing "a still small voice" at the end of the service and making one's way down to the minister during what were called the hymns of decision, hymns like "Just as I Am," and "Softly and Tenderly Jesus Is Calling." By going forward, one confessed one's sins "before man," i.e. the congregation. All of my brothers and sisters before me, when each was twelve or thirteen, had gone forward.

Long ago, my parents had decided that the Southern Baptist Church's doctrine, its literal interpretations of the Scriptures and its strict moral code, came close to their own Dutch Reformist beliefs, and since there were no Dutch communities in Jefferson City, they'd chosen the Baptist Church in which to raise their family. The Baptists were, in my parents' estimation, a somewhat rowdy bunch. The gossiping among the congregation before the service annoyed them, and the backslapping among the deacons who called one another brother and who sometimes sang out *A-men!* and *Praise the Lord!* in the middle of the sermon.

Certainly my family contributed to the raucous atmosphere.

We who were always late to services came in long past the opening prayers. Upon entering the sanctuary, hushed and ready now to receive the message, we traipsed down the aisle, all twelve of us, to take a conspicuous seat in the only empty pew on the front row next to the deacons. This was because my father preferred the early service. We must all be up and dressed and breakfasted by a quarter to eight each Sunday morning, a nearly impossible enterprise. The little ones, hurriedly dressed and/or dressing themselves, often forgot essential items; underwear, for instance. One Sunday morning my little sister Beth, who must have been about three, leaned over the pew to steal one of the pretty little gold pencils visitors were to use to fill out cards, and as she did so, her dress flew up, her bare bottom, at an unfortunately close range, mooning the minister. After the service, my mother suggested to my father that he should apologize to Reverend Nelson for the distraction. My father laughed. Maybe Reverend Nelson hadn't seen, he said. Or if he had, my father offered, maybe the Reverend thought Beth's fanny was just another bald-headed deacon.

It was something of an event those Sunday mornings when a member of our family went forward. My mother always cried, saying that nothing that child did now, no matter how bad, could erase his or her name from the Book of Life in Heaven. My older brothers and sisters had treated their conversions matter-of-factly. They'd made their way out of the pew with solemn dignity, had taken the minister's hand and stood stoically after the service as the congregation filed by to welcome them into the Kingdom. For me, however, going forward had been a disaster. I'd wept by the minister. Against everything in me I'd sobbed, my face in my hands, as the congregation filed quickly by. Why had I wept so? Maybe it had to do with my recent dismay over my breasts and the secret, humiliating fact

74

that only one breast, at first, had appeared. It would be some months before the other surfaced. In light of my weeping, my mother offered another explanation. "Satan must *wrestle* the Holy Spirit for some souls," she said, hugging me hard, and for days my brothers and sisters steered clear of me as though I had something they could catch.

During this time then, converted, one-breasted, I took to reading my Bible every night, choosing the passages mystically. Settled in my bed, my rose night-light turned down two notches, a kind of candle-glow effect, I'd close my eyes and open my Bible and run my finger down the page. Wherever I felt moved to stop, wherever the Holy Spirit wanted me to stop—in the middle of a passage, or, worse, in the middle of a long list of begats, as begins Matthew—I'd open my eyes and read what I considered to be my message, surely God's personal message to me that day. Then I decoded it.

Once I read, ". . . and it shall come to pass in the day of the Lord's sacrifice, that I will punish the princes and the king's children, and all such as are wearing strange apparel . . ." Strange apparel. God must be referring to a row instigated the previous summer by Gena. Gena had purchased, without permission, a two-piece bathing suit, and, yes, I had taken Gena's side. I'd stood behind her, as had Eva, Connie, and little Beth. We'd wept with Gena as she had pleaded with our father. Wearing the suit, Gena had kept measuring her pale midriff, holding up two fingers to show how little of her was revealed. Well, God had waited a long time to make his point, waited all through the summer during which Gena had worn, to the envy of us all, what our father referred to as "that G-string," waited into the fall and now the suit was stained brown from the lake water and stuffed in a drawer somewhere. In the end, it had been decided that since Gena bought the suit with her own money, money she'd made sewing sheets for the clinic, she could keep it, though our father—he wanted us to know—didn't like it. Each time Gena came down to the dock he jumped in the water.

Why had God waited? No doubt to show me that, once assented to, evil became an ordinary part of one's life. Now I remembered there had been fights among the girls, fights and tears, everyone wanting to try on the suit, even, after a while, to borrow it. I'd sneaked, once, into the bathroom, had put on the suit, tucking it here and there with diaper pins. Well, sometimes God's worst punishment was simply having the last word, of saying through the Scriptures and through my fervent applications, "Look at the mess you've made or were in league with making. Just look at what you've done."

After three days of detention, the parable of the ten virgins pierced my heart. It was all too clear. The wise virgins were the experts, and the foolish virgins the Hoods. By association I belonged to the latter category, though I knew I didn't even have their courage to steal, to wear stretch pants. *Because thou art lukewarm and neither cold nor hot*, said Revelation, *I will spew thee out of my mouth . . .* As for the oil in the lamps, or lack of it, that was simply a measuring of one's successes or failures in Home Economics—what, elsewhere, the Bible might call one's talents. I read on:

While the bridegroom tarried, they all slumbered and slept.

And at midnight there was a cry made, Behold the bridegroom cometh; go ye out to meet him.

Then all those virgins arose and trimmed their lamps.

And the foolish said unto the wise, Give us your oil, for our lamps have gone out.

76

But the wise answered, saying, Not so, *lest there be not enough for us and you; but go ye rather to them that sell, and buy for yourselves.*

And while they went to buy, the bridegroom came: and they that were ready went in with him to the marriage: and the door was shut.

I understood my message. Sitting at the long library tables with the Hoods, hadn't I heard Eddie Fisher singing "Someday Soon," and Frank Sinatra, "You're Just Too Marvelous for Words," just as surely as the five foolish virgins, who upon returning from the oil vendors, must have heard the laughter and the music from the wedding feast? And then the sound of the door slamming, the hard click of Mrs. Harris's high heels echoing down the corridor as she returned to us. *Verily I say unto you,* I read in her expression, *I know you not.*

I'll always remember the Home Economics suite. You remember the settings for the deaths of your beliefs. As I grew older I'd pause outside the Future Homemakers of America's display windows at the high school on my way to chemistry or biology class and admire the lit, glassed-in displays exhibiting crocheted pillows or needlepoint Christmas stockings, the various difficult shades of the poinsettia perfectly executed, red to deep green. The atmosphere of the science labs with, row on row, their vast stainless steel sinks, their file drawers full of petri dishes and test tubes and pithing trays were a travesty compared to my first ambition. The parallels were cruel, the memorization, for instance, of the dissecting kit's instruments, and the smell of formaldehyde that clung to your fingers no matter how many times you washed your hands.

It came to me one night that what the Old Testament described as *the abomination of desolation*, the slaughtering of unclean animals on the sacred altars, was not unlike that week's opening of the fetal pig on the biology lab's green linoleum counter. Wasn't it a defilement, a perversion of the original, sacred institution of the kitchen? And then at the end of class to staple a shriveled foot with a name tag, close up the body like a too-full purse, wrap it in plastic like a roasting chicken, and drop it in among the fifty or so others that bobbed in cloudy juices in a pickle barrel. And then you simply washed your hands, arranged your hair, using the scalpel blade as a mirror . . .

By the end of one week's detention I was grouped in Mrs. Harris's mind with the Hoods and, understanding this, found it to be a less humiliating position than stupidity or the prospect of trying to explain the complicated truth, the truth which would have betrayed my mother, her drawers, our strange society of heroes and heroines. For similar, loyalist reasons I'd recently stopped brushing my teeth before school. It made me feel closer to home to keep the taste of breakfast bacon in my mouth all morning.

Then, for purposes I've never fully understood, Mrs. Harris released me. Maybe it was because, unlike the Hoods, I did attend class and complete assignments, however poorly, though I never correctly drew the drawers. Or maybe my mother had called Mrs. Harris, accusing her of throwing lambs among wolves. "We're moving on to the sewing room," Mrs. Harris greeted me one afternoon as I was about to enter the library. "Here—" She handed me a pattern for the first assignment. We were to make an apron. "Now go pick out some pretty material . . ." My heart leapt up. My grandfather had been an apron maker during the Depression. Maybe it was in my blood. But when my efforts were exhibited the next week on the bulletin board as an example of what *not* to do, strung up as they were with dissecting pins and little red flags that read *Pockets off center! Crooked hem!* I simply narrowed my eyes as I'd seen the Hoods do and sneered and the tears miraculously receded.

And so I gained the approval of the Hoods, who applauded me that day, and who were kind to me from then on. For the rest of the year before most of them "got sprung," they offered me their protection from certain aggravating boys. I'd heard what they'd done to one Ronnie Brock who had the reputation of goosing girls on the stairs. They'd jumped him after school and held him down while the leader, Sheila Crumb, peed on him. Thus, when Ronnie Brock threw a fish at me out of Weir's Creek at a picnic—Weir's Creek was a sewer, really, and on warm days the smell was awful—and I shouted, "I'll tell Sheila!" he clawed his way up the bank, retrieved the fish where it flapped on the road and began stroking it. "Please," he begged, "don't say nothing to Sheila." Ronnie threw the fish in a long arc back into the water. His face went lean in fear. I felt sorry for him. Still I held him there a moment waiting. I felt my power. I thought I saw how both of us would age.

CHAPTER 10 THE CLINIC

The clinic and its grounds caught the arc of a hill above the river. It lay to the east of our church and just a few blocks short of the prison. The land on all sides of it was fairly preserved, even so close to downtown. A smokehouse still stood, and out back, a carriage house. Above its windows were stable latticing and rust smears from the old hinging. The clinic's colonial white brick facade faced north so that during the summer, particularly, as you climbed the wide front steps, you were nearly blinded by the glare. Patients waited on the porch in lawn chairs or chairs they'd dragged out from the sitting room. Because no one was allowed to smoke inside—this was primarily a cancer clinic—many of the men, sometimes one of their lungs already gone, puffed away on the steps or leaned against the columns between the window boxes full of tango geraniums. One man I remember smoked through a tube in his throat.

Doctoring in Missouri was a seasonal business. Many of my father's patients were farmers or the wives of farmers. Winter storms closed the roads into town after Christmas. Then there was the spring planting to contend with. But during the summer, before the harvests began, things were easier on the farms. The clinic's appointment books were full, too full. People came early in the morning and waited sometimes until late afternoon to see my father, who thrived on the activity, and who spent, complained his nurses as they tried to keep him on some kind of schedule, too much time talking in the examining rooms long after the physical or follow-up was complete. You could overhear almost everything that went on in those rooms since the partitions dividing them stopped some distance from the high ceilings, and my father's laughter reverberated from one booth to the next as he listened to his patients' jokes and stories about their animals, their in-laws, their wives and children.

The summer I worked for my father at his clinic, my duties, like my sisters' before me, included, first of all, wearing the hand-me-down nurse's uniform that made me, insisted my mother, look older and professional. The workday began with my father picking me up at the house after his morning surgeries at St. Mary's. If the operations had gone well he was in a good mood and came bursting into the kitchen, though we were already late for the clinic, to have a Coke or a cup of coffee with my mother and me. If things hadn't gone well—maybe the cancer, during surgery, had proved to be advanced, or maybe his scrub nurse had been rude or slow on the job—he simply lay on the horn of his Chrysler. My mother scooted me out the door and I ran, carrying my white buck shoes still wet from the polish, to the car. On those days my father and I barely spoke. It happened that I was in love for the first time that summer, and I often tried to finish letters to my boyfriend on the way to the clinic. He was away working on a ranch in Montana. On the bad days it was difficult to write because of my father's sudden turns and accelerations. He leaned hard, like a figurehead on a ship, over the enormous steering wheel, hitting the brakes with one foot, gunning the engine with the other.

The clinic's two nurses, Sara and Evelyn, were waiting for us at the door. They'd already put in a morning's work, Sara setting up the surgeries and balancing accounts, Evelyn executing the daily skin cancer X-ray therapies. Sara would follow my father into his office, informing him of any new crisis or change in schedule. Evelyn held back. She wore the ugly, lead-lined apron which protected her from overexposure to radiation. She kept a hankie in its plastic pocket and as my father and I came in, she had a habit of taking it out and blowing her nose. Maybe our arrival annoyed her. For hours she and Sara had had the place to themselves. They'd brewed several pots of coffee, leaned, chatting, against the door frames. Evelyn looked to be a little older than my father, say, in her early sixties. Her hair was pure white, and she kept it tightly permed and coiffed like the women at our church.

I came to understand Evelyn in the context of the church women who wore rayon dresses and corrective shoes, and who took it upon themselves, year after year, to teach the children of the congregation about Christian living, though their lessons were, by turns, excruciatingly boring or disturbing in the way they could announce, in the bright rooms of Sunday school, that Herod had all the boy babies under two years old slaughtered in Judea, that the soldiers had torn the babies from their mothers and run them through with swords. Therefore, Evelyn made an excellent nurse. She could be counted on to attend, without a trace of revulsion or sentiment, the sick and the dying. Neither the facts nor the manifestations of illness fazed her, but over the long run they'd made her aware of every worldly odor, stain, and blemish. "You've got a pimple," she'd greet me frankly, lifting her drugstore glasses to peer closely at my nose.

"Too much chocolate," she'd conclude and go back to work. Evelyn had what analysts call good denial.

The day my older son was born I had a nurse like Evelyn. "I think I'm ready," I kept saying to her who sat in the labor room watching a quiz show on the wall-mounted television and knitting something with horrid pastel yarn. Mostly she ignored me, but every once in a while, by her own timing, she'd lay aside her knitting and cross the room in her white rubber-soled shoes to check on my progress. "I think I'm ready," I'd whisper as another contraction took me. "Honey"—she'd shake her head and lumber back to her chair—"you gotta lotta work ahead of you." Evelyn was like the charwoman in Kafka's *Metamorphosis*, peripheral, vital, the one who did the dirty work and was disdained for it. One day Evelyn showed me how she'd altered her nurse's uniform so that it no longer had a waist. Now it zipped up the front instead of buttoning. She offered to do the same for me.

Though no one would have said so, Sara was the favorite. She was in her late twenties and had recently been married and so she talked easily with me, when we had a moment, on matters of love. We did so clandestinely, speaking in whispers, because my father was afraid of losing Sara to a family now that she was married. Sara understood this and was flattered by his fears. Now and then she tried to reassure him. "Leroy says I can work as long as I want." Sara would raise her voice so that my father, in passing, could hear. "And I sure plan to. I sure do plan to just keep on working right here. Best job I ever had. Besides, I didn't study my brains out for three years in St. Louis for nothin'," she'd say, touching her nurse's cap. It bore, in tiny embroidery, her school insignia. "These is the sixties, for heaven's sake." We'd hear my father's office door close. Then Sara would pinch me and smile.

Sara was tall and big-boned with short red hair and pale freckles. She dealt with the patients firmly and with humor, and she wasn't offended by the off-color jokes the old farmers often told us as they settled their accounts after their exams, nor did she give in to them, exactly. "Well," she'd conclude when they were finished and snickering, their eyes searching her face, "*that's* one for the books. Now you look here. Don't forget to take your medicine." The men shrugged like children. Sara never shamed the hypochondriacs nor condescended to the very ill. She knew by the nature of the handwriting on the cards the patients filled out and dropped through the slot on their arrival who should not be kept waiting and who would not mind waiting—those, she'd say, happy for a day off the farm.

She was gracious to the city fathers who came into the clinic. Sara received them like a hostess, with dignity. On the other hand she often hugged the farmers, pinching their cheeks on the way out and asking to be remembered to the five or six members of their family whose names she knew, every one. Sara had been raised on a farm. It gave her authority to chide the men for their missed appointments or their neglect of themselves, their wives and children. And they listened to Sara better than they did my father, who was right to worry about losing her. In fact Sara did leave the clinic a few years later when she gave birth to a second child.

Sara let me set a snapshot of my boyfriend on the desk where I spent most of my time on the phone making appointments and accepting accounts. It was also my job to prepare patients for their exams. I'd go to the waiting room door and call the name of the man whose chart I held, escort him into the back rooms, weigh him, take his blood pressure, and request a urine sample. Sometimes, if Sara said to, I'd take his temperature.

One of the symptoms of advanced cancer is a low-grade fever. For a while, I also took histories on new patients. Taking a history meant asking a patient a series of questions from a printout concerning childhood diseases, family illnesses and tendencies.

But after about a month, Sara told me I didn't have to take any more histories. Patients had complained to her and to my father that I looked too young to be answered on the more personal data. This made my father impatient with me and with those shy patients. He was used to delegating various, often serious medical tasks to his children. Whenever he went out of town, for instance, he put Eva in charge of transplanting tumors from one group of rats to another, a task she performed with skill as she etherized the already dying, lay them out on their backs on the glass-top counter in the lab. My father had taught her to carefully palpate their abdomens, still warm but without a pulse now, to locate the exact position of the tumor.

She'd focus the light, take the scalpel in her right hand, make an incision, and extract, in an efficient moment or two, the cancer. Eva was fourteen the first time she executed, alone, the transplants, a procedure she'd watched our father perform hundreds of times. Though it was not our father's habit, Eva always sedated the healthy group before she mashed with forceps in a petri dish the excised tumor and filled the syringe. As she injected the disease, she was careful not to puncture any major organs. She held the limp, live victim in her left hand, stroking its belly when she'd finished. Eva's transplants always took, and when our father came home, he and Eva would go out to the lab to survey her work. Once he brought her a special gift, a dark, luminous lump called a mobé, which he explained to us was actually a rare tumor grown in an oyster instead of the usual pearl, the gift he'd brought the rest of the girls.

Following the complaints about my taking histories, Sara, Evelyn, and I would hear my father in the examining rooms nearly lecturing his patients that all of his children were going to be doctors and nurses—in my case, he'd add, a medical artist—his tone implying that to this end he expected their full cooperation. I'd look at Sara in alarm. She'd wink and wave her hand. And sure enough, after a few days my father gave up and didn't mention it again. I was secretly relieved. On several occasions, as I called this or that person to be examined, I'd spot one of my teachers in the waiting room. I'd take Sara aside and ask that when the time came, would she mind taking care of him or her? It was one thing, I explained, to ask a stranger if he or she had *pain during intercourse*, or *blood in stools or while urinating*, and quite another to ask these questions of the man who'd taught me algebra, not one, I might add, of my best subjects.

During those particular exams I'd make myself scarce. I'd hide out in the kitchen or file X-rays in the basement. Evelyn took over the desk. She knew better anyway my father's extensive, complicated code concerning who should not be charged for an office visit or recent surgery. Evelyn took pride in this knowledge, was possessive of it, and had already shamed me for my ignorance. "You better ask your father what goes on here." She'd shaken her head at me one morning after I'd written up a bill for an old preacher. The man had backed up, hat in hand, and looked at the floor. Evelyn tore into small pieces the account. "Your father don't charge men of God." In fact officials of any religion, and missionaries, and doctors and nurses and retired teachers received free care, no matter the extent of their needs. There were also patients who simply could not pay— Evelyn knew who they were—and they weren't to be asked. These people often paid for their care in other ways. They might send foodstuffs to the clinic at Christmas, cured hams or sides of beef or huge jars of pickled pigs' feet or, one of my father's favorites, pickled beets.

Once a patient offered my father about twenty cattle which, with high hopes, he put to pasture in the orchard one spring. The plan was that the cattle would keep the orchard grass short, eliminating, claimed the donor, the need for tractor cutting, a tedious job which my father and brothers had to work at all summer. This would save time, and money on gasoline. In the fall, fattened on clover, the steers would be sent to slaughter. The patient claimed that my father would turn a nice profit. But soon after their arrival the small herd flattened the wire fences surrounding the property and wandered into the woods and onto Main Street, stopping traffic, though the drivers warned one another not to honk their horns for fear of starting a stampede through the Memorial Park across the street from us. It took my father and brothers most of a Saturday to round them up, with the help of our dogs, all of them mutts, but which displayed amazing cattle-herding skills that day the way they bit at the animals' heels and surrounded the cattle and drove them, at last, back through the orchard gate. Maybe they'd unwittingly had some practice since all four of our dogs were hopeless car chasers. They were especially addicted to Volkswagens. My father gave the dogs beef gravy on their food that evening and he took to wearing a straw hat.

But as summer came on and the trees produced first fruit, the cattle began bellowing night and day. "They fancy mating," my father, with jaunty authority, told the neighbors who called to complain and told us who appeared at his and my mother's bedroom door. We couldn't sleep for the racket. "It's got to be more than that," our mother insisted. "They sound absolutely *beside* themselves." So my father put on his bathrobe and hat and went out in the dark to look at his cattle. As it turned out, they'd been eating green apples off the trees. Their abdomens were painfully distended. Anyone who has ever eaten a green apple—man or beast—knows the sour pleasures of a spring orchard. Two or three bites, with the front teeth only, and it's gone, quenching your thirst and waking a lean greed. You fill your pockets, though you know what's coming. And sure enough, an hour or two later the cramps begin. You double over in the grass, roll, crawl under a tree, and squat to relieve your bowels, grateful to tears at each expulsion. Weak, sweating, you bury your excrement with onion grass and spread out in the sun. Maybe you swear you won't do that again. You empty your pockets, throwing the reserve at the birds or into the pond, where the apples bob like toys among the cattails.

Still, the next spring, there you are, impatient among the trees. You think it won't happen again or that the apples are riper, nearly ready, and since the body has difficulty remembering physical pain, is blessed truly with a profound forgetfulness— a phenomenon that links us, maybe more than we understand, to the other animals—you pick and eat. It was a miracle, the vet told my father the next morning, that none of his cattle had died. One by one, the vet punctured their abdomens with a long syringe to release the gas. They bellowed with relief over the hissing. Now they could not, he ordered, stay in the orchard another moment. After Dr. Burgess left, my father took his hat off and tinkered with the tractor all day to hide his disappointment.

CHAPTER 11   PROCUREMENT
AND ASSIGNMENT

Sent from the East Coast under the govern-
ment's Procurement and Assignment, in the early forties, my
father had worked at a state hospital for the poor in Columbia,
about thirty miles north of Jefferson City. He had been drafted,
really, as were many young doctors during the Second World
War, to serve in an area of the country that suffered from a
shortage of medical care. After the armistice, he'd tried many
times to return East, but the government wouldn't release him
from his assignment. He'd begun, maybe out of frustration, his
own private practice on the side. Finally he saved enough money
to buy the old mansion in Jefferson City—he did most of his
surgeries in Jeff because Columbia's hospitals were short on
operating rooms—and he converted it into his clinic. It opened
officially in April 1947.

During the clinic's first years, unable to afford to move his
family, my father commuted from Columbia and slept nights
on his waiting room couch under a huge print of an ocean,
open ocean, no shoreline in view. It was a huge picture executed
in monochrome greens to grays to black, the strip of sky above

the water overcast. The water swallowed light. There were no whitecaps. It was more like a mid-sea swell viewed at eye level. My father had bought the print in a junk shop in New York because the artist was Dutch, and he framed it himself with pieces of driftwood he'd found in the Ozarks. My mother argued with him for years about hanging that picture in his waiting room. She believed that its message was too dark, that it would alarm people who sat wondering about the lump in their breast, the thickness in their throat, the cough that wouldn't go away. He held out a long time but in the end took down the picture. It hangs in my writing room now. In this way my father never stopped talking about going, some day, back East. Growing up, we were probably unnaturally comfortable with the prospect of our being visitors, tourists, really, in Missouri. We believed, like our father, that we were easterners at heart. Yet eight out of ten of us were born right there, a thousand miles inland, by the river.

The clinic was exceptionally homey. Even the sheets on the examining room tables were colored pink, blue, and green. At the beginning of each summer my sisters and I went to work cutting out and hemming five dozen or more which we sold to our father, a dollar apiece. The place was furnished for the most part with antiques that he'd bought at auctions around the state and refinished himself. Currier and Ives prints cluttered the walls, and by the summer of 1966, my own paintings—huge awkward portraits of my favorite characters, Miss Havisham, Arrowsmith, and others—hung above the partitioned examining rooms. My father often pointed them out to his patients, adding that someday he knew I'd be a great medical artist.

Behind the clinic's four examining rooms there were also a minor surgery and two X-ray therapy rooms. The original kitchen at the back of the house now served as a lab, the counters lined with sterilizers, jugs of Zephiran and alcohol, various testing equipment, and on the little table by the pantry, my father's microscope. For years he insisted on doing his own pathology. Not until the seventies, when my mother came to work for him, did my father wear a white coat at the clinic. He was opposed, he said, to pomp. It was not unusual for us to point out over dinner the bloodstains on his shirt and tie from his doing, without a jacket, his own lab work. He took pride in his cheap suits, bloodstains and all, which he bought at a local discount chain. No matter what my mother's arguments, he wore seersucker in winter or rag wool in summer until those suits fell apart.

During the late fifties and early sixties my father's parents, when they came to visit, occupied the clinic's second story. At two different times both would need surgery for cancer of the colon, their disease stemming, my father believed, from their having drunk all their lives from the dye-polluted New Jersey rivers. But cancer of the colon happened to be one of his specialties. It's documented that until the forties surgeons all over the world often removed only cancerous portions of any particular organ, among them the large bowel, using a scraping procedure on surrounding organs and tissues, but leaving intact whatever the malignancy had adhered to, portions of the liver, for example, or the small bowel, or, in women, the ovaries and uterus. My father suspected that the poor cure rate for this type of cancer was due to the spread of disease into the cellular walls of what *appeared* to be perfectly healthy tissue. Scraping the cancerous bowel away from its adherents was not enough. Only through removing the accompanying organs and tissue would the cure rate rise, in his work, to around ninety percent.

And long before his parents had become ill, my father had invented an instrument which he patented under the title the recto colic-anastomotic clamp, but which he called, simply, "the gadget." The gadget made the necessity for a colostomy—in some types of bowel cancer, the collection of wastes outside the body, following surgery—obsolete, pulling together as it did, after the excision of the malignancy, the two parts of the severed bowel. The organ healed, then, internally. My father cared for both his parents, executed their surgeries, and saw them through to complete recovery. Both lived another twenty years.

CHAPTER *12* *FERRYMEN*

The clinic had its own peculiar rhythms. On rare days we began at ten and were finished by five. Most days, because my father came in late from surgery or because we'd had unforeseen X-rays and biopsies, we didn't get started until eleven or twelve, nor lock the door until after seven. There was no such thing as a lunch hour. In the pantry my father kept an old icebox stocked with a diet protein drink called Metrecal which he'd duck back to drink while he studied a slide. Sara and Evelyn sometimes sent me to the coffee shop down the street for sandwiches, but they did so secretly and we gobbled our food as quickly as possible when my father was in with a patient.

I often took my sandwich downstairs. Supposedly I was filing X-rays in the basement. I liked the basement—its ceilings, at their highest point, only about six feet, and the walls plastered and replastered so many times that there were no strict corners. There weren't any doors, only archways leading from one low room to another, like a crypt, or like a first-century house I saw once in Spoleto, Italy. Even the steps dividing the rooms were rounded, as though they'd been exposed to decades of weather, and everything—floors, ceilings, and walls—had been painted a shiny white. A dehumidifier ran down there twenty-four hours a day. The roar was disturbing when you first descended. Then you grew accustomed to it and were perfectly happy to hear nothing. In spite of the dehumidifier, bright green algae clung to the corners and climbed the walls in surprisingly intricate patterns, like ice on glass.

Once a city official had shown my father a document announcing that the clinic, whose several buildings predated the Civil War, had been part of the Underground Railroad. The document marked it as one of the way stations for fugitive slaves as they made their way north. But where had they hidden out? My brothers and sisters and I wanted to know and we combed the clinic and its outbuildings trying to find some evidence, a name on a wall, a relic, but the search was futile. Finally we speculated on the best hiding places. The carriage house's attic was a possibility. Though now there were stairs leading to a third story, a reinforced square in the second-story ceiling suggested a trapdoor. The other possibility was the clinic's basement, and we agreed that it would have made the best hiding place of all. The door at the top of the stairs was narrow and latched flatly against the outer wall. Some piece of furniture would easily have obscured it, a grandfather clock, for instance, or a hutch.

Now there were charts in the basement in huge green file cabinets on over twenty thousand patients, enough to populate a city. I felt safe among them, among the names only, their disease abstracted, understood in context to "birthplace," as each file read, and "number of children," and "occupation," and "mother's maiden name." Maybe it's true that we want, in some cases even require, witnesses to our pain in order to remember it, to maintain, in spite of it, a point of view. How we remember it might depend, I suppose, on the manner in which our witnesses register our suffering. Sara and Evelyn, each in her way, were champion witnesses to the clinic's terminally ill patients, Sara's skill emanating, no doubt, from her youth, her good nature, her recent happiness in marriage. She could make even the sickest patient laugh. She had a repertoire of stories. One in particular I heard her tell. It was a true story, she always insisted, holding up her right hand like a Girl Scout.

One fall morning, she'd begin, she was driving in from the farm to work. "For *miles*," she'd say, "I had to follow this old truck—that road's full of ruts—till I got to the blacktop. And guess what was in that truck? Pigs!" Sara pronounced it *pags*. "They was probably on their way to St. Louis to slaughter. I kept thinkin' to myself, now the doctor won't like it if I'm late. But it was such a pretty mornin'." Sara changed tone, touched her listener on the shoulder and grinned. "You know, frost on the pumpkin and all that, the sky real blue . . . all the fields cut down so you could see *forever* . . . I didn't mind so much. —But don't you tell the doc!" Sara laughed until the patient laughed, then she added flatly, "Couldn't pass anyhow.

"So there I was, just drivin'." The more Sara talked, the more she fell into a southern Missouri drawl. She squatted down by the appointment desk and held up her hands as though she were clutching a steering wheel. "Ho hum!" she'd sing, meaning time passed. "Well, then I got to noticin' this one little pig aworkin' his way up 'the others, climbin' up *way* at the back, just climbin' till he's on *top* of the bunch. *Then* he starts walkin', sure as you please, on the backs of all his brothers and sisters! I couldn't believe my eyes! And t'others just sorta looked up at him like they's sayin', *You's crazy!* And you know what he did? He walked clean over to the rail and all a sudden he just jumped right off! Right off the truck! Right off!" Sara clapped her hands.

"Well, let me tell *you*, my heart was goin' a mile a minute. And good thing I wasn't trailin' too close or he'd a landed on my hood! Leroy said, 'Let that be a lesson to you, Sara. You done good.' Now I swear I thought that little pig was a goner, but he just bounced! He bounced one time, then he got right up and ran off! Just ran clean off through the field. Never stopped for nothin'. I just sat there in my car *laughin'*." Sara shoved the patient a little and slapped her own thighs. By now we were all laughing, even Evelyn. "I thought maybe I oughta catch up to that old truck and tell the driver, Mister, you lost somethin'! But na-a-a. I didn't." Sara came close to reassure us. "I just figured if that little piggy was smart enough to get free, well, Lord, that's his business!"

Evelyn's skills as witness to the sick and dying had a different effect, no less admirable. Evelyn faced facts, and though they were sometimes devastating, she shook hands with them like a good sparring partner. "Lookie here," she'd say as Mrs. M. settled her accounts, Mrs. M., whose lab report following surgery showed that too many nodes were involved. Evelyn addressed all of us. "With what she's been going through and she remembered that recipe I asked for—when was it, honey? Two, three months ago?" Evelyn held the recipe up for us to see. "I swear," she turned back to the patient, "you're a trouper. Bless you, honey . . ." Evelyn's eyes followed her a moment. "What's next?" Evelyn would bark as Mrs. M. found her way out. At that point Evelyn might begin hauling the gallon cans of X-ray developer in from the back stoop. Evelyn smelled always of developer, a slightly sour, rubbery odor which she tried to cover throughout the day with Lily of the Valley cologne.

Years later, when I read my sons a story describing the ferryman whose job it was to row the dead across *the river of the unbreakable oath*, I thought of Evelyn. "How do I free myself of this task?" asked the ferryman of the good luck child. "I'm tired of rowing. I need a rest." "Next trip," advised the child, "when you reach the far shore, hand your pole to your passenger. Then jump off and run!" The only difference that I could see between Evelyn and the ferryman was that Evelyn wouldn't have asked the question. Evelyn had worked for my father for years and continued there another thirteen years until the clinic's close in 1983.

But that summer I began to explore every conceivable way of steering clear of the staff and the patients. I was revolted at the sound of my own voice, by turns cheerful, grim, or condescending. I found that I could stay in the basement for hours without anyone fetching me. This was because, not long before I'd come to work for him, my father had fired a nurse who'd been so overwhelmed with the caseloads she'd taken to simply stacking—in the basement's corners, on the top of the file cabinets—the X-rays ordered during the previous fall, winter, and spring. At some point she'd even given up labeling them. Since Sara and Evelyn hated the basement, I'd inherited the job of sorting through the stacks and picking out the anonymous bowels and chests and matching them with the appointment book records and chart entries. I'd try to match three or four a day, though whether I did so correctly, I never knew. Sara went over my work each morning. Still, the pictures fascinated me. I'd hold them up to the bright tube-lights and study the softened shapes. X-rays revealed the body as animal, ageless, save the white swirl in the lungs. The bowels, full of barium, looked like the meandering of a river.

Other times I'd hide out upstairs in what had once been a school for mentally handicapped children. By July everyone knew I was no good at assisting in minor surgery procedures.

I had a habit of fainting. Once a man had come in to the clinic and requested that my father remove a tattoo that read "Gracie" on his upper arm. The man wanted to remarry, he explained, but his fiancée refused as long as he wore his former wife's name on his body. The tattoo removal was a safe and simple procedure, my father told me, and an excellent one, therefore, for me to observe and assist with. I was to hand him the instruments as he worked. But long before the cutting began, I started swaying. I remember my father suddenly barking Sara's name, like one of his children's. Sara caught me as I fell over the patient. I'd been surprised at my father's reaction to my fainting. He'd laughed, not unkindly, that evening on the way home. It was OK, he said. Even my mother, as a student nurse, had fainted during her first surgery. "Think of the body as a machine," he'd offered. But the next time I was to assist him I fainted before the woman, who was to have a breast aspiration, entered the minor room. After that, my father's announcement to Sara to *prepare* the minor room made me ill. Then I'd excuse myself and head up the stairs two at a time to the school, which was set up on the clinic's broad, sunlit, upper west rooms.

The school had been one of my mother's projects. Before its opening in the early fifties, mentally handicapped children in Jefferson City were sent away to state institutions. This had disturbed my mother so that she'd organized a staff consisting mostly of the children's mothers and furnished part of the clinic's upstairs with old iron-latticed and inkwelled desks that she'd convinced the public schools to donate. We all had a hand in refinishing them. Out back, she had installed a swing set, a jungle gym, and a slide. She called it the Peter Pan School, and though the children's comings and goings through the clinic's working hours made life there difficult, the nurses, insisted my mother, weren't to complain, nor my father, and the school thrived. By the early sixties the numbers of the enrolled had climbed to such an extent that the city built the Peter Pan School a larger facility and began bussing students in from rural areas. But my mother left the rooms as they'd been, left the desks in neat rows and the walls covered with cracked and yellowing tempera murals of brilliant, soft shapes—animals and trees— like the positives of the X-rays in the basement.

During minor surgery procedures I'd sit at one of the desks and finish letters to my boyfriend until Sara or Evelyn came to get me. I always hoped it would be Sara. She made my weaknesses seem arbitrary. "Feeling better?" she'd ask. "Come on down now. We're finished. Your father's asking for you." She said it as if she didn't know what it meant. Evelyn, on the other hand, would appear at the door with her hands on her hips. "You better get yourself some smelling salts, girl, or you won't make it through the summer." She'd motion with her head. "You can get 'em across the street at Suttons'." One day Evelyn produced a little vial of salts for me from her apron pocket. I thanked her, but I threw them in the bushes on my way out.

When the front door of the clinic was closed in the evening, Sara and Evelyn could go home. I waited with my father, who needed to go over all the cases of the day and record on the Dictaphone in his office notes to be entered on each file. My father's office was austere and exotic. The heavy orange hopsack curtains were always drawn, turning everything a dusty sepia. The wall above his desk displayed his many degrees and photographs of his favorite teachers. There were also group shots of the missionaries he supported standing in front of a jungle hut or waving from a canoe, some of whom had been beheaded in the fifties in New Guinea. The other walls held paintings which he'd smuggled out of Haiti a few years back—brightly clad people dancing on a shoreline under the flag of the Republic, these next to African masks and wall hangings from Yucatán, and a few of my own paintings, the gypsies of Crete, which I'd copied out of *National Geographic*.

My father's desk took up the east side of the room. I'd sit down in the cracked leather chair—the chair patients sat in during consultations—next to the bookshelves, the ledges of each lined with human bones he'd dug up here and there, obsolete surgical instruments, Aztec and Mayan sundials and figurines. But each time I picked up one of the objects to examine it, my father would be torn between his dictation and telling me the story of how he came to own the relic I held, so that I learned to leave them alone. The stories were long and detailed and since I didn't dare interrupt him, we might not get home, those evenings, until after eight.

As I scanned the relics or the photographs and paintings, my father described each case of the day and offered, one by one, a prognosis or diagnosis. I'd try to put the names he spoke aloud with the faces I remembered, and I listened for the word *mass*, the first in a sequence of more specific descriptions that often, over the weeks, arrived at the words *sarcoma*, or *carcinoma*. "Mrs. L. has a pea-sized mass," he would begin, "in her left breast, about one centimeter from . . . this morning it would not aspirate . . . Sara has scheduled her for a biopsy on Tuesday morning, at which time we'll do a frozen section . . . X-rays today showed evidence of calcification . . ."

Listening to my father each evening, I learned that the cooler his tone, the more likely he believed the mass to be serious. After a while I took this approach, too, with my father, with Sara and Evelyn, and with the patients. As I ushered them into the examining rooms I found myself using a more formal, a more comfortably distant diction. Would they *disrobe*, I'd ask, adding that *the doctor* would be with them *shortly*, and did they *require* a magazine? "Listen to her, would you?" Evelyn exploded one day, but Sara shushed her. I must have believed that my reticence made me less conspicuous, by my own logic, less complicit, if only in their memory of the day they'd walked, worried, into the clinic, and walked out again onto the high white steps, the facts of their lives altered.

Now they would come to know the clinic well, the world reduced to the ritual of first the biopsy, then the surgery, then the lab reports indicating how many nodes involved. We'd come to know them too, know their families, their children and grandchildren who played on the clinic's front steps or out back in the Peter Pan School's weedy yard, while inside in one of the partitioned rooms, my father marveled at such a beautiful, well-healing scar. He'd call us in to see, and we would praise those patients for taking such good care of themselves, praise the relatives for their excellent care of their mother, their wife, their husband or father. You could hear us all over the clinic as we reassured and celebrated. Then we let it go. My father wished them well and said he knew they hoped they wouldn't be seeing him for a while—at least until their next follow-up with tests —and that he didn't, laughing, take it personally.

Maybe that evening his dictation would confirm a good chance of survival. Or maybe it didn't. Too many nodes involved, or surrounding organs and tissues. So began, if possible, a series of radiation or chemotherapy treatments, the latter of which could only be administered in Columbia. This meant months of trekking back and forth from one town to another for treatments which made them ill, took their strength, their hair. Sitting at the appointment desk where, with Evelyn's help, I'd map out therapy schedules on a series of cards, I'd write *September* and imagine the look of things as the leaves turned, the window boxes on the porch filled with marigolds. Then I'd write *October* and *November* and see someone coming in a strange light up the steps, a few dead leaves in the crevices. Finally I'd write *December*. In December my mother would have hung an evergreen wreath on the door. In the waiting room there'd be a Christmas tree and Sara would play carols on the hi-fi. I liked writing *December* down. If the patient made it that far, it must mean the therapy was working. Sometimes, when Evelyn wasn't looking, I'd flourish that card with a holly sprig or a star.

CHAPTER *13* IMPRINTING

I don't remember the name of the boy who drove me one August evening to the Zeeland cemetery. He knew where it was, only nine miles from Holland, Michigan, which was his hometown. It was Saturday. We had a couple of hours before my train left at midnight for Chicago. He pulled the car up close to the wrought-iron gates and left the headlights on to make it easier for us to read the headstones. But the cemetery was bigger than I'd imagined, maybe a half mile deep into surrounding fields, so that we decided, to save time, to begin at the opposite ends of each row and meet in the middle. Farther and farther from the headlights we got down on our hands and knees and crawled from grave to grave, searching the names, like braille, with our fingers. We were trying to find Rena, Aurie, and Genevieve Van Dyke, my maternal grandmother, grandfather, and aunt, my mother's older sister, who'd died at birth, and whose name, with slight revision, had been given to my mother.

Maybe I thought that if I found them, the fact might appease my parents upon my arrival the next evening back in Jefferson

City. From Chicago I'd fly to St. Louis. Then I'd take the Greyhound home. During the previous week I'd called my parents every night from a pay phone in downtown Holland, begging to be allowed to return from the small liberal arts college they'd sent me off to with high hopes, and no doubt, relief, in the late summer of 1968. Hope College was famous, they'd learned, for its excellent anatomical art instruction, a prerequisite to graduate studies in medical art, and since my high school grades and entrance exam scores hadn't been high enough to find me a place in their alma mater in Wheaton, Illinois, Hope was, they reasoned, a sound alternative.

The activity of their having chosen a college for me hadn't been completed without my protesting, without tears, grandstanding. I had my own ideas about where I'd like to study and I'd sent off for applications. When my father refused to sign them or forward the necessary fees, I'd run away from home, and for five days in February I'd stood my ground. Nights I slept over at the carriage house behind the clinic. My sister Rena had taken up residence there because her husband, that year, was on a Navy destroyer off the coast of Vietnam. Suspecting Rena of harboring a fugitive, my parents cruised the alley above the clinic after eight each night, or they dropped in before seven in the morning. But Rena and I always had a hunch. We saw them coming. Twice, out of a dead sleep, I leapt up from the bed Rena and I shared and sprinted down the narrow stairs and out the back door to hide in someone's car. When the coast was clear, I'd make my way back, hugging the walls of the buildings, in my nightgown and bare feet.

I was hardly home during that winter and spring anyway, except to sleep. School started at eight and I was busy each evening until after seven with operetta practice. At the end of January, to my great joy, I'd been given the lead in *The Music Man*. I was to be Marian the Librarian in the spring production.

But my happiness over having been given the part was to be my undoing. On the fifth day of my self-imposed exile I found a note on my locker from my sister Connie. *Please come home, Deb,* it read in Connie's childish hand. *Please or something terrible will happen. Dad's threatening to call the director to say you can't be Marian. I only wanted to warn you. Listen, Deb, I'm on your side* . . . Poor Connie. She was always seeking me out, appearing suddenly before me at some forbidden party or pulling up next to me in the family car at the drive-in to say *Hurry! Come home! They've found the cigarettes in your room* . . . *the bourbon in the Listerine bottle* . . . *they've found the letter and* . . . *they've read your diary and* . . . *hurry! Come home!*

I suspect now that my parents would never have made that call, but by the late sixties we'd all gone unpredictable on one another. Besides, they had their reasons, though no one at the time would have dared to mention what they were. Gena and Eva, my two sisters directly ahead of me in the lineup, had a few years before broken ranks, had not, though each was accepted, gone to Wheaton, as had Everett, Paul, and Rena. Instead, Gena had made application to a small Baptist college just outside Kansas City. Maybe she'd paid the fees with her own money. Of all of us, Gena was the most resourceful.

One summer day when she was just fifteen, she'd marched into the National Bank and, opening her own checking account, deposited the two hundred dollars she'd been accumulating, money she'd made sewing sheets for the clinic or baby-sitting or weeding the gardens. Having opened the account, she returned home to clean out old clothes, baby furniture, tractor parts, bushel baskets full of toys from what was loosely called the maid's room, though we hadn't had a live-in maid for years. Gena sorted it all, labeled boxes with Magic Marker, and dragged them down to the road for the Goodwill Industries.

That accomplished, she proceeded to move her clothes, her

bed and dresser, desk, lamps, etc. into that little room over the garage, a room inaccessible to the other bedrooms since to get to it you had to descend the main stairs, walk through the front hall, the kitchen, and through a door that led up another flight of stairs. At the end of the narrow hall was her new room. Then Gena took the bus alone to the hardware store and wrote a check for two gallons of powder blue paint.

The new room had a little bath and sink and toilet which Gena scrubbed down and disinfected. Wearing one of our father's surgical masks, she spent a day chipping lye out of the spigots while she soaked the drains with acid. Eva and I watched every detail of the process with awe. "What a great idea!" we chorused. "Why didn't we think of it?" But Gena wasn't moved by our flattery and she wouldn't let us help for fear we'd make claims on the room. "Let's get this straight." Gena's mouth moved under the mask. "You come up here by invitation, understand?" In the years to follow, Gena sometimes allowed Eva and me to "sleep over," make popcorn in a machine she'd purchased, drink soda from a cooler she kept in her closet, and listen to the top forty on the radio while she polished our nails with apricot pearl polish. It's worth mentioning that Gena was responsible for introducing to the family the portable hair dryer, tampons, and the taco.

For these reasons, and because of her excellent grades and entrance scores, Gena had been allowed, against tradition, to attend the college of her choice. Eva, two years later, did likewise, selecting a small girls' school in Columbia. Had the story ended there, maybe all might have gone well for me, too. But after a year at William Jewell, without warning, Gena transferred herself to the state university at Columbia. There she dropped any pretense of studying nursing and enrolled in acting classes. She took a job as a bank teller and moved into a studio apartment. Once Eva and I sneaked up to Columbia to see it. Gena's one-room apartment included a Murphy bed, a tiny bathroom and kitchenette which Gena had decorated with tiger-striped curtains and matching tablecloth. During the summer Gena even managed a trip to Europe and sent home postcards from Athens, Rome, Paris, and sun-streaked Polaroid snapshots of herself and a group of long-haired strangers playing in the fountain at Piccadilly Circus.

Eva's experience was different, no less dramatic. Eva more than successfully completed her freshman premed requirements, but she dropped out after a year to elope. I wrote Gena with the news in care of a family in Berlin. I hoped she'd come straight home. *Too bad, honey,* she answered me from Venice. *Don't let it get you down. Hey, take the maid's room. I give it to you* . . . In either case, my parents blamed themselves and the world, which to their way of thinking became more unmanageable each day.

Every night Walter Cronkite had nothing but bad news. At the dinner table we assigned ourselves to silence and watched our parents' faces as they, in turn, watched footage of soldiers loaded onto stretchers by the hundreds. During the Tet Offensive in the late winter of '68, the casualty lists were the lead story, followed by scenes of Berkeley and Columbia where students, bloodied on screen by policemen's nightsticks, chanted obscenities, their faces veering wildly before the camera. Then the report switched to Watts or Harlem or Washington, to smoky night shots on the new color television, to glass shattering, to George Wallace, before the primaries, mugging, *Is this the face of a bigot?* under the Dixie flag. In the spring came the assassinations, King in April, Kennedy in June. Our parents watched it all over chicken and gravy, pork chops and mashed potatoes, chuck roast, steak and french fries and apple sauce, and we watched them and registered each crisis by their mutual outcries or silence. Who were any of us to argue that the world wasn't a dangerous place, wasn't immoral, when *Hair* opened on Broadway in April, when "Mrs. Robinson" climbed to number one on the charts.

And whether it's peculiar to large families in general, or whether it was peculiar only to ours, the pressures on the ten of us to conform, indeed, our abilities to do so, were equated with our sense of personal safety, even, by some stretch of the imagination, with fair-mindedness. At best it imposed a structure in the midst of chaos. "Your sister was paid five dollars for twenty sheets, and so will you be for your twenty," our mother would say when one of us tried to collect more for our labor. Or sometimes we won the argument. "Gena got to have a two-piece bathing suit when she was my age!" Eva, Connie, Beth, and I each sang at the beginning of our fifteenth summer.

At worst it erased particularly you. At fast-food stands our father always ordered for us ten hamburgers, ten bags of fries, ten small Cokes. It was the Old World speaking, some trace of the prewar European in his blood, only one generation removed, which insisted on so predisposed a standard, a standard, whatever its content—daily bread to the college he chose for us—created during his immigrant's son Depression boyhood through which, since nothing was certain, everything was plotted. My father's notions of democracy tended toward the literal, surrounded as they were, like a ship breaking the horizon, by vastness. For him the pursuit of happiness meant catching glimpses, now and then, of a future against whose big sky he could herd his dreams. "Ten hamburgers," he'd say proudly, as if at last he could execute the script he'd written for himself years ago, "ten bags of fries, and ten small Cokes, if you please, young lady." We who listened had the feeling that destiny backed up behind his words.

To interrupt him, then, with your own petty tastes was to interfere with destiny. Any dissenting requests for a cheeseburger, a bag of onion rings, a shake, were naturally ignored, and if you couldn't keep quiet, held against you by the herd instinct of your brothers and sisters. For example, maybe by speaking out you confused the waitress so that she did send up on top of the uniform order a lone cheeseburger, a stray shake. And say that not for arbitrary reasons of a need, suddenly, to announce yourself, you seized them, claimed them at great risk to be yours, and gobbled them up in a moment.

Believe me it came back to you who had, now, your autonomy. Your sisters and brothers, envious or bored, would take to calling you the name your father, upon doling out the orders, had called you, *hornswoggler*. All day you would be *hornswoggler*. You would be it in every game of tag or hide-and-seek, a spectacle of selfishness, ostracized, a dream smasher, the last to be served at supper, the last, before bed, whose prayers were heard. So that day by day of your childhood, week by week and year by year—save a few times when you found yourself, you'd swear against your will, chanting *cheeseburger-cheeseburger-cheeseburger*—you learned the perverted freedom, the anonymity inherent in conforming, learned how to be invisible, how to be left alone.

But alone I hadn't made it through Hope College's freshman orientation. When I arrived at the dorms I put my luggage in my room and went out to wander the little town of Holland, taking note of every pay phone and coffee shop, the laundromat, where, as the days progressed, I read through the stacks of old *Woman's Day* magazines. That week the movie house ran a Doris Day Festival. The matinees began at two and I planned my life around them. The first afternoon I saw *Calamity Jane*, and the next, *Don't Eat the Daisies*; then *Move Over, Darling*; *Pillow Talk*; and *By the Light of the Silvery Moon*. Other features ran each evening but I avoided the movies at night. Terror, like other emotions, seeks contrast, something to tell it who it is. Better to move out of the dark theater into the four o'clock light just in time for dinner, a hamburger in the coffee shop.

Around seven I'd walk the few streets over to the train depot and study the schedule. Two trains left daily for Chicago. On the weekends there was only one train and it left at midnight. Rarely was there anyone in the station except the ticket attendant and he was hidden from view in a little cage of an office. He ignored me as I spread out each evening on the wide wooden bench, like a church pew, and dozed. As it turned out, the depot became the only place I could sleep that week. Maybe that's why I remember it so well, remember its precise layout, the border and re-bordering of black and white tiles on which, by my bench, several gray gum spots emitted a minty odor.

On the other hand, I remember my dorm room not at all, though I lay awake there night after night and must have watched the walls whiten as the sun came up. I couldn't say today on what floor you might find that room, nor would I be able to identify even one distinguishing feature belonging to my roommate who lay in the bed next to me, nor what, if anything, she said to me or I to her. Maybe the fact of being able to sleep, therefore wake up somewhere, allows for a sort of imprinting, the way some animals at birth imprint on an object, machine, another animal not of their genus, simply because it's the first thing, upon opening their eyes, they see.

After a few hours' sleep in the train station I'd open my eyes on the fan turning slowly above me, the ceiling inlaid with plaster roses, and sit up, reassured that the door to the platform was propped open by its pickle jar full of pennies. Some train or other would soon be in. Maybe no one would get off or board. But there would be people on the train going somewhere, maybe home. Car by car, the lights would be on. Stalled at the station or racing over the countryside, whether you could see them or not, they would be on. It made me stronger to think of it, hopeful enough to walk to town and make another call to my parents.

Our conversations went something like this. "Hello, Dad? Dad, this is Debbie. I need to speak to Mom." By Wednesday they'd tired of my calling so that my father would answer, "Your mother can't come to the phone just now, Deb. What is it?" "I want to speak to Mom, Dad. I have to speak to Mom. If you hang up, I'll call again . . ." "Honey?" My mother picked up the extension. "Honey—" she'd repeat, but as my father slammed down the phone, her tone sharpened. By Thursday she no longer bothered with preliminaries. "Now you listen to me, young lady. You're staying right where you are."

"I can't, Mom. I'm sick or something. I can't eat, Mom. I can't sleep . . ." Confessing to her in this way made me cry. "I have to come home, I have to." "Have you gone to the health center there?" "Yes," I lied. Illness in our family wasn't legitimate unless it had been confirmed, and it couldn't exist without documentation, a chart. "Well, what did the doctor say that you had that you should be sent home from college? What did he call it? Give me the name of the doctor and I'll call him myself." "Forget it, Mom. I didn't see any doctor." "Aha! I thought not . . ."

But caught in a lie, I got out the big guns. "I've got the money," I said. "Dad's check cleared yesterday. I've got five thousand in cash . . ." "How could you?" my mother gasped, but she answered too quickly. She'd anticipated this, my taking my tuition money hostage. "I haven't paid the fees yet. I'll use it," I threatened. "If you won't let me come home, I'll go live with Eva . . ." "Everett!" my mother barked, not bothering to place her hand over the receiver. My ears rang. I hardly heard my father pick up his extension.

"She's threatening to live with Eva . . ." To hear my mother speak of me in the third person was comforting. It made her oddly responsible, in the way she'd always been, for her girls. "For heaven's sake!" my father exploded. "The money's cleared," I chimed in. "How could you?" My mother began to cry. We sobbed in unison. By Friday they relented. "Come back the way you came," my father instructed. He absolutely would not let me talk to Mother. I had a little speech prepared in which I promised to work at the clinic for him for free, but he cut me off. "Don't think you're going to lie around here for the rest of your life," he finished. "I got you in at William Jewell." "Dad—" "Classes begin Tuesday."

I don't remember much about the rest of that evening or the next morning, save dragging my trunk at noon to the depot and buying a ticket for the midnight train. Then I spread out on my bench and fell asleep. A stranger shook me carefully awake and brushed the hair trailing saliva from my mouth. I sat up groggy and embarrassed. Maybe she'd awakened me because my skirt had ridden up over my hips and my underwear showed. I adjusted my garter belt and smoothed my skirt over my knees. "What time is it?" I asked, accepting her handkerchief. "A little after five. Are you waiting for someone?" How did I answer her? Did I tell her my mother had suddenly become ill, or my father? Did I suggest by my shyness that it was a subject not to be pried into? I know I didn't tell her the truth, that I was, for reasons I couldn't understand, incapacitatingly homesick. To have tried to explain would have meant bumbling into a chain of family fears, and if I knew nothing else by my eighteenth year, I knew that the secrets my family lived with demanded my loyalty, their syllogisms, my allegiance, even when their premises were faulty. So what if they were like a slow virus kept in check by our mutual silence? I told the woman a lie, something we both could live with. I was good at that.

She was a pretty woman, a little younger than my mother, with dark coiffed hair. She looked professional, and sure enough, "I've just come from Grand Rapids," she told me. "I had a little business to take care of." She turned around to study the schedule, her hand resting on my shoulder. "But your train doesn't leave for hours," she said. "Were you aware of that?" I feigned distraction. "You're worried," she concluded and smoothed my hair. "Have you had supper?" she asked, then answered herself, "You're coming home with me. My son will bring you back to your train when it's time." She stood me up and called to the man in the booth to watch my trunk. Truly I didn't want to go with her. In light of my lie her kindness shamed me. Still, I let her lead me to her car.

And that's how I came to meet the boy, say his name was Nick, who drove me later that evening to the cemetery. What distinguished him was his leanness, his army haircut. It made him look older than he was, though as it turned out he was exactly my age, born, like me, in 1950. He was as restless as I at the supper table and didn't have much to say except that he'd spent the summer at boot camp. In a few weeks he was leaving for Vietnam. To fill the silence as we cleared the table I mentioned that I had relatives buried in Zeeland. Maybe to get out of the house for a while, Nick seized on it. He insisted on driving me there, helping me find the graves, though we never did.

After about an hour of looking we gave up and he drove me to the depot. I wish I could say that we laughed about something and I said good luck and he, same to you. I wonder if we'd recognize each other now, the way, say in an airport, you spot someone who looks familiar and he looks at you with the same puzzled knowledge, though you don't speak. I wonder if he made it back. We shook hands on the platform and he waited around awhile outside the train. Maybe he thought it was polite, or his parents always did that. I pretended to read until he went away.

My train pulled into Chicago's Penn Station the next morning before dawn. The lobby was deserted except for a few travelers slumped on the benches. The skylights were dark and someone was waxing the floors, the whir of the machine swallowing the click-click of my high heels across the swirled surfaces that, from the top of the stairs, took on the aspect of ice, or history, someplace swept so clean it's hard to imagine there was ever a wedding, ever dancing. "Hope you're not in a hurry," the taxi driver greeted me at the exit. "No," I said, "no hurry," as we cruised slowly through Chicago, now and then swerving over the curb to avoid the debris that littered the causeways.

"Hold on," the driver warned as he stopped short to let a half dozen policemen on horseback cross in front of us. "What's going on?" I asked, but he ignored me. The driver opened his door and waved to the officers who broke into a gallop toward what looked to be campfires along the lake. "What happened?" I repeated. The driver snorted. "What happened? Well, where you been, little lady? Shit." He spat as he got out of the cab. "Go get 'em!" he called after the police. I could see people scattering where the horses reared and lunged through the crowd. Someone darted in front of us and the cabby leapt back in his seat and threw the car in gear as if to run him over. I watched the boy scale the overpass, then turn to throw a rock at us. It hit the hood and bounced off. "Bastards!" the cabby swore and laid on the horn. It was September 1, 1968, the Sunday morning following the Democratic National Convention. "What's going on?" I tried again. The cabby stepped hard on the gas. "Read the papers, girl," he said as we sped down the parkway to the airport.

CHAPTER *14* WISHBONE

Whenever I've traveled from Missouri, no matter how close to sea level my destination, I've had the feeling of being up high. This is true whether I'm driven or drive myself or take a train. Oddly enough, an airplane trip is the least disorienting, though I do feel set down on elevated ground, especially if, on descent, I have a view of a coastline. Once, driving at night through the flatlands of Wyoming, I thought the road must be up dangerously high. I was afraid I might go off the shoulder. It occurred to me to stop the car and walk out onto the plain to prove to the animal in me that we were safe, but the notion of standing still on so high a place seemed doubly fatal—as I sped along, it was as though I were instigating the turn of the earth—and I drove fast toward daylight.

We sang about it in church, fear of falling, falling from grace. My King James Concordance lists over a hundred references to *fall. n.; fall. v.; falling. n.;* then on to the word *fallow.* From angels to people to cities, you might say falling is an Old Testament obsession that carries on figuratively into the New. In the second temptation of Christ, the devil transports Jesus to the highest pinnacle of the temple and taunts him, "Cast thyself down: for it is written, He shall give his angels charge concerning thee: and in their hands they shall bear thee up, lest at any time thou shalt dash thy foot against a stone." In the ancient Hebrew texts there are listed nine orders of angels, the highest being the Seraphim, known above the others for their purity, and having three sets of wings.

In 1942 in the region of Dordogne, a dog fell into a hole in the ground and its owner crawled in after it. The boy saw that the walls of the shallow cave in which he found himself were covered with pictures of animals, ponies whose shaggy coats were the stalactites, and bulls whose muscular haunches swelled along the rock. Deer antlers overlay a horizon across which distant herds grazed, each scene a wash of pigments made from pollen, dirt, flowers, blood. Deeper into the cave in what is now called the crypt or holy of holies, archaeologists discovered a stick man on the wall floating in right-handed composition above an eviscerated bison, the spear piercing the animal through its anus, emerging at its genitals, the entrails dangling as it falls to its knees. Levitating or falling on the diagonal, the stick man hovers, his phallus erect. To his right is a spear or a staff upon which is mounted a bird. The man wears a mask beaked like a bird.

Critics, as Joseph Campbell tells us, argue about the meaning of this particular painting, some insisting that it's simply a hunter slain by a bull and memorialized. Others say that the man figure is a shaman "rapt in a trance," this idea born of the artist's association of the man with the bird, "with wizard flights in ecstasy whether to the underworld, to the heavens, or to those realms beyond the horizon from which shamanic powers derive." In either case it appears that even in 15,000 B.C. we were disturbed by the imagination. It made us stick figures among the other animals. We worried that we weren't two-winged. Neither are we two-armed, exactly. Unlike the other animals, humans are for the most part right-handed. The first stone tools—rocks sharpened on their left sides—illustrate that early on Homo sapiens practiced left-brain maneuvers, the left brain responsible, as well, for chronicling time, understanding the relationship of the past to the present and the present to the future, something like *the tool I made yesterday I can use today and tomorrow*, something like *I go to prepare a place for you* . . . Darwin links early man's skill with his hands to the development of language:

> To throw a stone with as true an aim as a Fuegian in defending himself, or in killing birds, requires the most consummate perfection in the correlated action of the muscles of the hand, arm, and shoulder, and further, a fine sense of touch . . .

> The structure of the hand in this respect can be compared with the vocal organs, which in apes are used for various signal cries, as in one genus, musical cadences; but in man the closely similar vocal organs have become adapted through inherited effects of use for the utterance of articulate language . . .

> *In my father's house are many mansions* . . .

Recently scientists have discovered that birds, like people, have a left and a right cerebral hemisphere. It's believed now that their songs are learned, are not, as previously thought, mere manifestations of instinctual or genetic instructions. Birds have been recorded to sing, in fact, in dialect. A northern and a southern sparrow trill a slightly different series of notes. And Darwin suggests, in *The Descent of Man*, that sleeping birds, like people, even dream, this "shewn by their movements and the sounds uttered." He cites Jerdon's *Birds of India* in which the author quotes a man named Houzeau who claims that his "parakeets and canary birds dreamt."

As winged things, are birds' nightmares of rising instead of falling? And thus, would angels fear the same terrible weightlessness born of their possessing wings? The single characteristic that separates true birds from flying reptiles is what is called the wishbone, not unlike the sternum or breastbone in humans. In Genesis the serpent in the garden says to Eve, "Knowing good from evil, ye shall not die, ye shall be as gods . . ." Did the serpent, himself a fallen angel, have a wishbone?

CHAPTER *15* LOTTERIES

One May morning in 1971, the morning before the largest antiwar demonstration the University of Missouri campus would see, my husband, Charlie, tried again to warn the colonel. "I understand, sir," Charlie said into the phone. "I wouldn't have bothered you if I weren't concerned." Charlie motioned for me to take our one-year-old son, who was banging his spoon on his tray, into the other room. I lifted little Charlie out of his high chair but I danced him around our kitchen. I wanted to listen to the conversation. It was news to no one but the colonel what was about to happen. I'd heard about it weeks ago in the Art Department: the Students for a Democratic Society, which until recently had seemed virtually nonexistent on the University of Missouri campus, threatened a violent protest during the annual R.O.T.C. Spring Parade. Rumors circulated that people from out of the state, from California and New York, were coming to Missouri to help organize it. The stories worried me. Charlie was Group Commander of M.U.'s R.O.T.C. unit. He'd heard the stories too, and he'd attempted to convince his superiors to cancel the parade.

Ever since the Cambodian invasion in 1970, small, peaceful demonstrations had taken place all over campus. There were the Silent Vigils, for instance, each Thursday at noon outside the Student Union. Once a week, winter through spring, I'd stood in line with the protesters, many of them friends of mine from the Art Department. We held candles to represent the casualties of the Vietnam War, though in the February and March winds, it was hard to keep the flames lit. The R.O.T.C. Honor Guard, presenting the U.S., Missouri, and Air Force flags, stood at attention on the opposite side of the Student Union steps, most of them, like Charlie, victims of a low draft number.

The atmosphere of those early vigils was friendly. After the first draft lottery, it was understood that the protesters were the lucky ones. Most had flunked the physical or their numbers were over two hundred. Many were women. In the eyes of the Rotcies, the protesters, in our blue jeans and parkas, were the embodiment of a lost opportunity, while the Rotcies, in their Air Force blue, their short hair and government issue shoes, were like some dream confrontations which by a fluke of the body—a missing vertebra or high bilirubin count—the protesters had awakened from. As we straddled the dirty snowbanks off College Avenue under a clock that didn't work, though the bells in the tower sounded twelve, then one, 31,000 troops were loading onto ships or planes on their way to Vietnam. During those vigils I always tried to get in line directly across from Charlie so that we could wink at each other without his breaking attention. Sometimes one of the protesters brought along a transistor, and by the tinny voice of Janis Joplin or the Rolling Stones, Charlie would shrug a little and smile, as if to show me he was dancing.

The eerie memory of the TV broadcast lingered in which the birthdays of all eligible men had been fed into a hopper to be pulled out by an official. Like some crazy quiz show, the birthdays, year by year, had gone up on the wall, 1947, 1948, and then 1949, Charlie's birth year. Charlie and I had sat in front of our tiny television in our apartment in Columbia, the telephone between us. I was about seven months pregnant. Each time the phone rang, it meant one of his friends' birthdays had just been called. The consensus was that if your number was under 100, you'd be drafted for sure; 100 to 200 was tricky. But over 200, you were safe. We didn't have to wait long during the 1949 drawing. Charlie's number came up: 69. There was no way, after his graduation from college in the spring, that he could escape the draft.

For some of our friends, going to Canada was an alternative. A number of seniors had already begun planning the trip north. In the days following the broadcast I brought up the possibility many times. But Charlie insisted that it was not in him to leave the country in order to dodge the draft. "I just couldn't, Deb." He'd close down the discussion before it got started. "Then we're sitting ducks," I'd answer. "No, no." He'd smile and pat my belly. "Listen, I've got a plan." The best we could do, he explained, was for him to join the campus R.O.T.C. unit. Joining R.O.T.C. would give us and our baby—who was to be born in May—more time in Columbia. In that year after his graduation, he could begin law school. "Maybe by then the war will be over," he'd assure me. If not, at least he would enter the military as an officer.

Charlie and I had been married in August of 1969 during the week of Woodstock and almost a month to the day after Armstrong had landed on the moon. We'd had a big church wedding in Jefferson City. My sisters had been my bridesmaids and over five hundred guests had attended. We'd held the reception at Orchard Acres, setting up many little tables among the apple trees. Standing for hours in the long receiving line, my family

—all of us present—had met most of Charlie's family, aunts and uncles and cousins from all over the South. His only living grandparent, his dead mother's mother, had traveled from Tennessee, and Charlie and I kept excusing ourselves to bring her cups of punch where she sat on a love seat we'd pulled next to the door.

We'd met during my senior year in high school, not long after my sister Eva had eloped, in the old-fashioned sense of the word: farewell note, ladder, late night escape, and all. She'd actually climbed over the balcony above the kitchen one May evening and into her future husband's arms. I missed her. The fact of her absence angered and amazed me. I lost my appetite and had trouble sleeping. My chronic diarrhea I treated with paregoric, which my parents kept on hand in the medicine chest in their bathroom. The opiate in the medicine always lifted, briefly, my spirits and I suppose I became addicted to it, substituting, when my bowels began cramping, phenobarbital.

That summer I had some accidents with the family car, the worst of which transpired when I ran a stop sign at the intersection by my old grade school. I was hit, broadside, by another car, the impact knocking me out of the driver's seat and onto the floor on the passenger side. I watched the sky skid past as the car drove itself up the curb and over a row of shrubs before it stopped, perfectly centered, between the Sinclair gas and the stop signs. No one could open the doors, and for some reason I refused the gathering crowd's pleas that I climb over the seats and let myself out the back of the station wagon. I just sat there looking up at the faces as they mouthed sympathy, asked questions, and as time went on, commanded me to answer them. Not until the tow truck came and pulled the car from between the signs and my father opened the door did I spring up to wrap my arms around his waist.

For the next few days, under some kind of sedation—Doridon, maybe, or Nembutal—I dreamed a blue sky filling with faces. I wept in my sleep and called for Eva. Sometimes I'd wake to find my mother leaning over me, or my father. "Eva," I'd say again, mostly to worry them. I could see that my mother had been crying. One morning early I woke clearheaded and hungry, got myself up, and went down to the kitchen. My body ached and I relished the pain. I stretched carefully to feel it stun me. I ate several ham sandwiches and a couple of sweet rolls and when my stomach revolted, I stood over the sink and retched and watched the sky turn pink over the fallout shelter. Then I went back upstairs and bathed and dressed, and no one spoke of the accident again.

I began running, as my mother put it, with a fast group of seniors. We called ourselves the Big Eight, and we packed into a girl named Helen's new red Firebird, which had an Italian horn that sort of warbled; you knew it anywhere. Armed with a bottle of gin we'd stolen from some parent's liquor cabinet or paid an older brother or sister to buy for us, we drove wildly around Jefferson City, or climbed, three or four of us, into Helen's trunk to sneak into the drive-in movies and harass the couples who were making out. By then I disobeyed my parents in most matters. I scoffed at their religion, and though there was no way of getting out of going to church and Sunday school each week, I stayed in bed until the last minute. My mother would leave me the keys to the second car so that I could follow them. I didn't dare miss altogether, but I'd take my time, driving slowly, smoking cigarettes through the empty downtown streets. I'd douse myself with Chanel before I joined my family in the front pew. In fact I was sorry to have missed the hymn-singing part of the service.

But I didn't go any longer to Sunday school. I'd hide out in the girls' bathroom until I knew classes were in session, knew my parents and four younger brothers and sisters in their various classrooms stood *with heads bowed and eyes closed* for opening prayer. Then I'd tiptoe down the corridor and let myself out the back door of the Educational Building. If I had the car I'd drive across the bridge and beyond the rural crossroads on my way to Columbia. I loved the road to Columbia that meandered through the bottomlands along the river; the bluffs on that side jutted straight up from fields that grew winter wheat and black-green alfalfa. At Columbia that road met Interstate 70. You could go east, free and clear, to St. Louis or west to Kansas City. I could get as far as Ashland, a tiny town halfway to Columbia, before I had to turn around and gun the station wagon at 85 or 90 back to church.

If I didn't have the car, I'd walk, as Eva and I used to, to the bus station and sit reading, drinking black coffee at the counter. I was a big Faulkner fan that year and had set a course for myself to read everything he'd ever written. This was mostly because my father disapproved of Faulkner. Often he'd leave books by my bedside table, biographies of the famous men of medicine, Lister or Pasteur, which I promptly returned to his bedside. Besides, my reading made my mother nervous, especially after Eva had eloped. Reading suggested secrets, collusion with a text. At the lake house, through the summer of 1967, when everyone was down at the dock, I'd stay up with a book on the porch. "Deb!" my mother would call to me every fifteen minutes or so. "Honey, come on down and join the family! We *miss* you!"

In late October of '67 Charlie arrived to pick me up at the carriage house behind my father's clinic where my sister Rena was living. That year Rena's husband was completing a tour of duty on a Navy destroyer off the coast of Vietnam. Charlie's and my date had been arranged by a friend who went with a freshman at the state university in Columbia. I was forbidden to date college boys, and Rena wasn't happy about my using her place to rendezvous. "If Mom and Dad find out," she warned me, "they'll never let you stay with me again. Think about that." Rena had just turned off the recorder, my father's huge reel to reel, on which she made hour-long tapes to her husband. Sometimes when I stayed with her I'd wake to her voice as she described for Cal how she'd fixed up the carriage house or how her job was going at a local grade school. Rena had a light, childlike voice, and it hurt me to hear her, all alone, speaking to the air. "They won't find out," I assured her. "Can I say hi to Cal?" "No." "Can I wear your green bellbottoms?" "No."

But when Charlie came to the carriage house door, Rena's attitude changed. In fact both of us grew shy in his presence. He was strikingly handsome. He smiled easily and in doing so communicated a dignity, an authority. His voice was sympathetic and sure. He introduced himself as he stepped into the room. Charlie wore a tweed jacket, dress slacks and shoes. Rena and I exchanged a look that said we understood he *had breeding*; as our mother would have said, sophistication. When he smiled again Rena wiped her hands on her jeans and tried to smooth her hair. "Well come *in*," she answered. "You must be looking for Debbie . . ." She sounded disappointed.

Things changed, at least for a while, after I met Charlie. I took stock. I felt better. I stopped taking the paregoric and only occasionally went for the phenobarbital. I even tried out for a part in a school play and got it, the part of Mary Warren in *The Crucible*. Something about her character fit me. She was a liar with an imagination. Play practice began each day after school and ran until about six or seven. After practice Charlie would pick me up at the high school and we'd go park somewhere and make out until eight. He always brought me a hamburger and fries and he'd watch me with an almost fatherly satisfaction as I ate. On the weekends he sent me flowers—not just flowers, but red roses, twelve each Saturday, with a card that read *From a secret admirer.*

My parents wondered at the roses. "Now, who is it?" my mother would demand in the kitchen as she helped me dump last week's dead bunch in the trash and arrange the new ones. "Just some boy I met at Helen's," I'd answer. "He liked me. I can't help that." "He wants to come to the play," I added one Saturday. "That's nice." My mother jumped at the chance for information. "Who is he?" "He goes to the university." I tried to sound casual, sisterly. "Forget it," my mother returned, dropping a rose on the counter. "Well, no one can stop him from coming to the play. Anyone's allowed." Mother sighed and I stole a glance at her. She looked older these days, tired. I was aging her. The fact turned me hard. "You can't stop him," I said as I picked up the huge vase of roses and left the kitchen. *"Free and open to the public,* remember?"

The night of the play, I watched from the wings as Charlie found his way through the crowd to my parents. He looked like one of the adults, like a citizen. He was wearing a coat and tie. I saw him remove his gloves as he introduced himself and shook my father's hand. Like Rena, my father backed up a step—the way he did when one of his children said something clever—and my mother took off her glasses and put her face close to his. I watched Charlie, at my mother's insistence, follow them to a seat in the front row. Charlie cupped my mother's elbow and it seemed to me she was blushing. It was my best performance. Never was Mary Warren played with such conviction, such energy. When she broke down in the juror's box, when she looked up suddenly, directly into the lights that made her eyes fill with tears and described the dark forest, the coven, the brilliant, the beautiful face of the devil, the audience sighed. My parents gave me to Charlie that night, as they would give me to him over and over during the next thirteen years, as they still, a decade after our divorce, try giving me back to him, though he has remarried and so have I, though he lives in Missouri and I in Massachusetts, not far, after all, from Salem. During the curtain calls I watched my mother's face, my father's. My father smiled back and as I looked on, he put his arm around Charlie as though he were one of his children.

We had been married a month when I became pregnant. Charlie was a junior in college that fall, and I should have been a sophomore. But I'd flunked out of William Jewell the previous spring, the spring of 1969. For the year my grade point average was .25, the quarter of a point because I'd gotten one A—in a painting class—out of twelve F's. The trustees' hands, they would write to my father, were tied. Mine was the lowest grade point on record, and the record went back over sixty years. It happened, they would console him, that every now and then an individual was simply not ready for the rigors of academic life. Perhaps this was the case with his daughter.

I'd had, by late sixties midwestern standards, a wild year at William Jewell. Having arrived at school a week later than the other freshmen owing to my trip to Michigan, I felt out of place, and I hated the campus on sight, the pretty little quad on top of a hill in western Missouri, the earnest faces of the students and their enthusiasm to draw me out. Already many of the girls in my dorm were meeting nightly for Bible study. I refused their invitations and avoided the lounge where they congregated after ten in their nighties, Bibles in hand, and sang their favorite hymns. It was bad enough, I'd tell them, to have to attend chapel every morning. Though they were stunned by my words, I saw too late that I'd given them a project. Soon after they took to leaving notes on my door, quotes out of tracts written by retired ministers in the home office in Jefferson City, ministers who'd attempted to "modernize" the Gospels in order to make them accessible to teens. *I'm so glad that you are here,* one note read, *it helps to see how beautiful my world is,* or *Jesus was the flower child of God.* The notes were flourished with happy faces or daisies.

One night, unable to sleep, I was pacing the halls when I passed a door to which a note was taped, a note identical to the one I'd received that morning. *Today,* it read, *is the first day of the rest of your life.* Through the door I heard music, a single voice singing, *I met a boy called Frank Mills on September twelfth right here in front of the Waverly, but unfortunately—I lost his address . . .* I thought it was a record, but when I knocked, the music stopped and a red-haired girl in a black negligee opened the door with a guitar in her hand. "OK," she said, not bothering to take the cigarette out of her mouth. Her left eye twitched at the smoke. "OK, I'll stop, just don't report me again, huh?" "I'm out of cigarettes," I said. "Can I borrow one?" "You don't *borrow* cigarettes," she said and let me pass.

Susan always wore a huge black wool cape that had deep pockets from which she'd produce a bottle of Bacardi as we walked the dark streets of Liberty, Missouri, to the parking garage where she illegally kept a car. By then the dorms were locked. We'd removed the screen from my first-floor room and shinnied ten feet down a drainpipe to freedom. Susan and I would pass the rum back and forth as we drove the thirty miles or so into Kansas City to an all-night club called Skipper's, a basement hangout with black lights and strobes and live bands who invited anyone in the audience to sing or play along with them. I met many people, some from William Jewell, some from the art schools nearby. "He's 4-F," or "He's 2-S," Susan described the men she introduced me to, as if the fact that they couldn't be drafted justified their presence at the bar, explained their carelessness, their wild dancing. "What's our status?" I shouted across the table to her one night. I thought it was a good question. "Flunkies," she mouthed, and took a serious drag off her cigarette.

At Skipper's I met Ray Keenland. I knew who he was before Susan introduced us. He'd been in his senior year at a school nearby. Apparently he'd dropped out to protest the war. His father was a minister in a small town in Missouri, and it was thought that because of this Ray could get C.O. status. "He's going to get a job in Appalachia or something," Susan shouted over the band. Ray glanced at me and looked away. "I'm going to California," he corrected her. "Really?" I said. "Soon." Ray nodded. "Real soon." Ray was good-looking. His brown hair was to his shoulders and he wore a red bandanna around his crown that made him look exotic. He had a full beard and a large, broad nose and a way of keeping his head always slightly raised, nostrils flared. I was attracted to him, mostly, I think, because I knew I bored him. "So what's your thing?" he asked when Susan went up on stage to sing with the band. "Painting," I answered, too giddy. He feigned mild interest. "Abstract or what?" "I like to paint people," I said. "Not portraits or anything . . . you know, groups," I corrected myself, "studies." "Drag, man," he croaked, catching his breath as he took a hit off a joint. "You oughta go abstract. You know Pollock?" "Who?" "Jackson Pollock, man. He just *threw* paint on the canvas." Ray dumped the full ashtray on the table and blew, then swept the ashes onto the floor with his arm. "Like that," he said, and turned back to the stage.

During the weeks following, I ignored Charlie's messages and stopped writing to him. I went with Susan every night to Skipper's, slept through all my classes except Painting I, which began at three. Though we were supposed to be working with a female model, I abandoned my early attempts to see and record. Instead I painted floating breasts rising from an oil-wash blue. I worked on huge canvases, stretching my own, charging hundreds of dollars' worth of arts supplies at the bookstore. At the end of the term there was to be an art fair and I knew Ray would be there. During the winter show just before the end of the semester, Ray bought one of my paintings, a large orange to black planet from which hung various parts of the human anatomy, even the internal organs, which I was especially good at, having copied them, all through high school, out of *Gray's Anatomy*. I was especially good at pairs of anything, the ovaries, kidneys, testicles. I loved their symmetry and shaded them carefully to give them a baggy, global effect.

I watched Ray making his way along the displays inside the Commons, stopping now and then to peer closely at the canvases, at the terrible landscapes and river scenes, the life studies done in black and red. He seemed to be studying technique. I was disappointed to see the painting he'd bought, a still life—wine bottle, dead flowers, some fruit—apparently attempting to echo Picasso's blue period, the drape behind the objects like a crazy waterfall. When he finally came to my booth, he backed up and blinked many times, as if to allow my paintings to dawn on him. When he said nothing, I tried to stand, but he put his hand on my shoulder and held me down. "Ya." He grinned slowly and took me in. "Ya," he kept saying, nodding. He went for his wallet and placed five dollars in my hand. I didn't have the heart to tell him the price of the painting was thirty dollars. I'd spent that much on turpentine. "Come here, baby," Ray opened his arms and hugged me, lifting me off the ground.

Once in his apartment, Ray set his new purchases against the wall and we made sudden, single-minded love. As he pulled off my jeans I tried to find my balance on his waterbed. The black rubber mattress, half exposed, was patched in places with bright plastic, like an inner tube. Ray saw me looking and he pulled an Indian throw over the spots. "Go with it," Ray whispered as I flailed. He tried to smooth my hair. His thumb caught in my ear. "Ouch!" I grinned. "Sorry." He wouldn't meet my eyes, but I saw myself as he must have seen me, awkward, leggy, and as he kissed me I laughed.

Charlie was waiting to greet me on the platform just before Christmas as the Greyhound bus pulled in to Jefferson City. I turned my face so that his kiss caught my hair, and I backed up so that he'd have to acknowledge my appearance. Instead of the pretty blouses and skirts of the year before, I now wore paint-stained blue jeans and one of Ray's shabby turtleneck sweaters. And I'd dyed my brown hair a blue-black. Parted on the side, a stiff sheath covered one eye. But Charlie wasn't appalled as I'd hoped he'd be. "You look great," he said. "New look, huh? I missed you so much. I'm glad you're home." My parents weren't so generous. But they held their tongues as my mother, no doubt, had suggested. They received me at the back door of the house with a reserved silence, but they hugged Charlie and fussed over him until I actually felt jealous. Most of the vacation I stayed in my room listening to the sound track from *Hair*, coming downstairs only for meals or to watch for the mailman in order to intercept my grades. When they came, I destroyed them and the letter from the dean placing me on probation. "I have a library fine," I lied when my mother began wondering. "They hold grades until you pay. I did OK, really. B's and C's. I'll do better next term."

Susan didn't return to school second semester. I didn't know what classes I'd signed up for, and I practically moved in with Ray. We'd spend the days making love, sleeping, or driving out into the country to the mental hospital farm where Ray used to work. The employees and patients liked Ray and they let us exercise the horses. I was a little afraid to be alone with Ray in new situations. It was like him, once we left the stables, to gallop off, leaving me to find my way back over the fields, the narrow paths above the river. Once I had a horse that kept returning, no matter what I did, to the barn. This angered Ray. It ruined his game of losing me. The fourth or fifth time the horse headed back, it broke into a run, then tried to buck me off at the gate. Ray followed us back, leapt off his horse and picked up a piece of fence about the size of a two by four. Then he hit my mare across the head. Ray ignored my horror. He simply pulled me out of the saddle, mounted the stunned animal, and yanked hard on the reins. "Take mine, goddamnit!" he shouted and headed off toward the river.

Charlie began driving up to Liberty, even on week nights. He'd catch me at my dorm as I waited for curfew and bed check, after which I'd climb, alone, out my window. It was already past eleven but my housemother liked Charlie and she bent the rules for him. "What's happening?" he pleaded one night as we sat in his car in the dormitory driveway. "I'm seeing someone else," I said. "Who is this guy?" Charlie returned, amazed. "I'd like to meet him. Listen, I'll get us a room at the Howard Johnson's tonight and we can talk about it. If you can climb out the window for him you can do it for me." "I better go in," I said. The housemother was signaling, turning the lights off and on. I was exhausted, hung over. And that morning Ray had told me he was leaving the next day for California. The draft board was after him, he said. They'd refused to give him a C.O. status. He'd just been notified he was 1-A. Ray said he was going to hitchhike to California. He was almost out of money and was soon to be evicted.

"Why California?" I'd said. "Why California?" he'd mocked me. "Baby, you don't know anything." He'd shaken his head as he took apart the kitchen, packed pots and pans. He even took the little sign off the baseboard that read NO PARTIES AFTER TEN. ROACHES WILL BE EATEN. Ray's kitchen was overrun with bugs. "I'll give you rent money, Ray," I'd said, "or I'll go with you." "No way, baby." He'd laughed, but he'd turned to look at me and I saw he was considering my offer. "I guess not," I answered quickly and began on the dishes. Something had occurred a few nights before. Ray had sat in his dark apartment in wait for me to walk in. I called his name, looked in the bedroom to see if he was asleep, then I'd gone into the kitchen to make coffee. I was just sitting down at the table when Ray had leaped, howling, out of the broom closet. I'd been so frightened I'd dropped my full cup, and covering my face with my hands, slid silently down the wall. Ray stared at me a few moments. Then he grabbed the filthy dishcloth and began wiping at the coffee. It was one of those cheap, thin towels that merely spread the mess. It came up black and dripping. Ray tossed it in the sink. "This proves my point," he'd said, lighting a cigarette. "This was a test . . ." He mocked the Civil Defense broadcasts. "See what your reaction was? Passive, man." Ray snorted to himself and turned his head. I hated it when he did that. It was as if there were a league of men behind him laughing, too. "What am I going to do with you, baby? You always look like something's about to happen to you."

Around four the next morning, about the same time Ray was preparing to hit the interstate, I woke in my dorm. It seemed foreign, empty, like a hotel room. I went into the bathroom and opened my mouth and gagged from the pain. Later, in the infirmary, the doctor looked worried. "You have a pretty bad case of strep throat," he said. "The worst I've ever seen. You should go to a hospital." He called my parents and by that afternoon I was home in bed, drugged, falling in and out of sleep. Sometimes when I woke, I thought I saw Charlie sitting by my bed. "I'm here," he'd say. He looked beautiful, healthy. He'd take the washcloth from my forehead, swing it around to cool it, then replace it. I thought I heard him speaking to my parents outside my room. But when I woke the next morning, he was gone. "I thought Charlie was here," I whispered to my mother. It hurt to talk. "He *was* here," she said. "He had classes this morning. *He* never misses," she said, but in a moment she was sorry. "He'll be back this afternoon." She sounded happy. "He has a surprise for you. Wouldn't you like to get fixed up a little?" "Mom," I hissed, "for God's sake . . ." "You don't need to swear." She sighed and handed me the pills.

Charlie came back about six. He appeared in my bedroom holding a dinner tray. "Try to eat a little something," he said. "I can't," I whispered. "What's the surprise?" "Your mom." He smiled. He liked to say the word *mom*, I knew; his mother had died two years before. Charlie looked nervous. He set the tray on the bureau and sat down on the chair by my bed. "Listen," he began, "I know it's been a rough year for you— for us. But—hell." He reached into the pocket of his sport coat and produced a little velvet box. We heard a rustle outside the door. My mother was eavesdropping. I tried to swallow. "Ugh!" I grunted and sat up a little. "I love you," Charlie began again. "I love you and I—I don't give a rat's ass about—you know." "What?" "That guy, that Ray. Do you?" "Oh, that." I tried to sound casual. "Not really." I lay back again and closed my eyes. I thought about Ray. He was through Kansas by now. Maybe he'd made Denver. Something went through me and I wished suddenly that I were with him, even though I knew I didn't love him, or him, me. With Ray I'd been anonymous, no one's sister or daughter. I fought the feeling, conjuring Ray's face as he'd hit the horse, leapt from the closet, what he'd said. *You always look like something's about to happen to you . . .* "Debbie—" Charlie's eyes were earnest, afraid. "Will you marry me?" "Will I what?" I croaked. I was trying not to laugh. It felt like the times I'd been caught red-handed at something— lying, or smoking in the bathroom—some occasion in which the evidence was so obvious, there was no recourse but to admit my guilt. "Don't try to talk anymore." Charlie put his fingers to my lips. "Don't." He laughed with me. "It's OK," he said, and I let him slip the ring on my finger.

The R.O.T.C. Spring Parade that May afternoon in 1971 did turn ugly, but there was no real violence, no National Guard. The flag bearers' dummy guns were without bayonets. Since Kent State, people took precautions. And maybe the S.D.S. members from Berkeley and Columbia never arrived. But I was glad I hadn't brought the baby to see Charlie, the Group Commander of the Spring Parade, hold attention while protesters— some of them friends of ours from the Art Department, friends from the vigils—spit insults in his face, even shoved him or got behind him and tried to buckle his knees. Standing with a group on the hill overlooking the field, I caught sight of a painter friend ahead of me in the crowd. Sometimes he held the baby for me during the Silent Vigils on Thursdays. I called to him but he ducked away and disappeared, as if I'd broken some code of anonymity, a code that said you weren't to recognize anyone or remember anything up until this moment, a code insisting that today you were without a history. Later I watched him stoop and pull up a handful of grass and sprinkle it on a Rotcy's head. "You're dead meat, man," he said and moved on.

Across the huge lawn in front of the Administration Building demonstrators lay down and the five hundred or so Air Force Rotcies picked their way ridiculously over them, marched forward in staggered formation, turned sharply and marched back. By May in Missouri everything is in bloom and the grass is a deep green. The field, bordered by gardens full of tulips and daffodils, was a violence of color, the dress blue of the Rotcies clashing with the red and yellow bandannas, the Indian-print shirts of the demonstrators. But the protest seemed to be taking place without a volume that would match the action, as if the sound of the afternoon had been turned off, as if the whole thing were merely a rehearsal, or the restaging of a memory and the participants were tired of the script. Now and then one of the Rotcies would trip and fall over a protester to be hoisted up by companions. Between the columns that centered Peace Park, a woman unrolled a Nazi flag, and then the grounds were overrun by strangers, men in suit coats with cameras, supposedly the FBI. A few fistfights broke out. The Rotcies began running off the field. As I was leaving I saw that someone had tried to start a bonfire in the street behind the law school. A small crowd fed it with papier-mâché effigies of soldiers, but the fire kept going out. "Hey," one of them called to me, "got a light?" Because of the way I was dressed, he'd taken me for an ally. I tossed him a book of matches and paused a moment as he tried again. I wanted to say something to him, explain myself, Charlie's position. But I was already late to pick up the baby at the sitter's.

CHAPTER 16 *A LONG RECEIVING LINE*

Charlie soloed in a Piper Cherokee the morning before we were married. As part of the ritual, his instructor cut the tail off his shirt, and Charlie gave it to me on our wedding night. Later, we framed it and hung it in our living room. Charlie loved to fly and we figured it was in his blood. His father had flown in the Korean War, and his mother, a little woman just five feet tall, had taught Navy pilots how to fly in World War II. During our first two years of marriage we lived in Columbia. Charlie finished college and began law school, working for his father's insurance company after classes. When he was sent out on farm inspections, he'd swing by the dress shop where I worked, pick me up, and we'd drive out to the tiny airport just outside Columbia and take a plane up. It was expensive, and a lot of the money the two of us made went to pay for his hours toward his private license.

I loved to fly too, loved riding next to Charlie over the fields, catching the thermals above the river. I've heard people say that to them small planes are the most frightening. "In a prop," they insist, "you feel every bump, every air pocket." But I prefer

138

planes like the ones Charlie and I flew because of their lightness. Under our feet a few inches of metal were all that separated us from the sky. We tested the currents and navigated by them. The updrafts buoyed the wings and pitched us left or right. Charlie caught those wakes and we'd swoop down close to the fields as he told me stories about how this or that pilot had recently flown—illegally, of course—through the St. Louis Arch, or under the bridge on Interstate 70 where the Missouri and the Mississippi rivers meet.

Charlie taught me the phonetic alphabet—the transcription of each letter in the alphabet into a word—the code that, internationally, pilots use to identify, over the airwaves, their craft. *A* becomes *alpha; B, beta; C, charlie;* and so on—*delta, echo, foxtrot* . . . I loved the worldliness of the call signs—*W* translated *whiskey; T, tango*—and what seemed to me their arrogance, or maybe it was the way Charlie said each word aloud. "OK, *indigo, juliet, kilo,* say them, *victor, whiskey, x-ray, zulu* . . ." Charlie had a strong Missouri accent. His mother had been from the South, and like her, he often gave words more syllables than they seemed to have. "She used to say *wawada,* instead of *water,*" he liked to tell me. In this way he pronounced *delta* as *dealta,* or *whiskey* as *wheiska.* Sometimes he'd give the controls to me. As late as three days before I had the baby we were up in a plane trying stalls and restarts midair. "Like this," Charlie would show me, pitching the nose of the plane high and easing back on the fuel. Then the nose would fall forward. The engine would sputter out. For a few seconds everything was quiet. You could hear the wings cutting the air. "Wait!" I'd plead when he reached for the start button. "Not yet!" and we'd glide a few more seconds. After the baby was born, he went up with us, too.

.   .   .

139

We called the baby little Charlie, just as his father had been called, and his father before him. Our baby had the Roman numeral VI after his name. His was a fairly easy delivery. I woke one morning to find that my water had broken in my sleep. The contractions began a little while later and when, by the book, they were about five minutes apart, we left for the hospital. Charlie wasn't allowed to sit in the labor room with me, and that afternoon he'd had to leave the hospital to take a final exam. Eva, who was living in Columbia with her husband and three-year-old, passed me notes while he was gone. *How ya doing, baldy?* she wrote. *Hang in there, baby. Mom's here, now,* she wrote. *Hi, darling,* I read in my mother's hand. *It'll be over soon,* and, *This is the day they give babies away with a half a pound of tea . . .*

But I was feeling angry with them both. No one had told me about the shaving, the pain, the total lack of privacy. Not my sister, not my mother—who'd had ten babies—not the books I'd pored over for weeks. In Missouri at that time, there were no such things as birthing classes. I'd had a tour of the hospital, a chat with the nurses, a peek at the newborns. That was my preparation. *Why didn't you tell me?* I wrote back to them. *I'm sorry,* returned Eva. *Be brave,* from my mother. *You'll forget all about it.* But I didn't forget about it. Once in my room after the birth, I greeted them both coolly. Eva looked anxious. She'd sneaked in against the rules to give me a quick hug. She giggled as the nurse escorted her out but I could see I'd hurt her.

As for the baby, he seemed like a stranger. I couldn't connect what I'd carried inside me with this little person. The events seemed unrelated. "Can't we take him back?" Charlie half joked with me the first night the three of us spent in our apartment. If the baby even whimpered, we shot up and tried to feed him. Then we changed him, changed his nightie. In a few days,

Charlie was off to O.C.S. and I was alone with my new son.
I'd never been much help to my mother with my younger brothers and sisters. Mostly, I'd competed with them for her attention.
Now I had a baby of my own and he scared me. I'd lay him
out on my lap and stare at him, try to place him, and he'd look
back at me, his dark blue eyes trying to focus on my face. I
cared for him, all right. And I took lots of pictures of him with
the Polaroid, as I knew you were supposed to, and sent them
to his father, who was training in Oklahoma. I pored over Spock
and subscribed to baby magazines, but I felt like a fraud. I cried
myself to sleep each night at my lack of maternal feelings, cried
through the two and six o'clock feedings.

One day, as I was rocking Charlie on the swing at my mother's, we both dozed off. I could feel the baby begin to slide from
my lap and I almost let go. The sound of the cicadas lulled us,
and the sound of the tractor in the distance. My little brothers
had taken over the orchard, cleared it of dead wood, planted
new trees. I woke and peered down at the baby sprawled on
my lap. A spider was crawling across his face. Something stood
up in me. I grabbed the baby and brushed so hard at the spider,
I smeared him across Charlie's forehead. Then I raced into the
kitchen to wash him. "What happened?" My mother stepped
quickly back to let me pass. "A goddamn spider," I said over
the baby's howling, "had the nerve . . ." "Let me take him,"
Mother ignored my swearing and tried to take Charlie, but I
held on. "No, no," I said. I was surprised at my deftness as I
held the baby under my arm, turned on the faucet with one
hand, tested the water with the other. I watched myself take
efficient action as I wet the corner of a dish towel and dabbed
at the smear. "I don't think he was bitten . . ." I said. "Here,
let me," my mother tried again. "I've got him," I said. I held

Charlie up in front of me and looked hard at his face. We recognized each other and I spoke to him, not in the silly baby talk I'd been practicing, but directly, calmly. My mother stood back, watching. He stopped crying. And for the first time he broke into a goofy smile.

CHAPTER 17 WATERWALKERS

After the baby was born it came to me: *We die alone*. Giving birth had been the first thing I'd ever done by myself. No one could do much to help. No sister could step in at the last minute and take over, and there was no postponing the event. Ridden down the hall from the labor to the delivery room, I'd watched bystanders watch me. I'd been instructed to resist the urge to push the baby out by way of a shallow panting. It was hard work and I concentrated, though I saw myself as they saw me, my legs propped wide under the sheet, my back arched as the last long contractions took me. The bystanders—nurses, aides, new mothers along the corridor—held me in their surprised gaze as they backed against the wall, then turned to other things.

"She looks too young to be a mother," I heard one of them say, as if she could dismiss the spectacle of me by way of the observation. Or maybe she said it out of sympathy. Nevertheless, even as I was wheeled out again, emptied, triumphant—the baby just under me since I'd been turned on my belly—as I passed my mother and sister and Charlie in the hall, all of them patting my back, my mother crying, Charlie trying to get a peek at his son, I couldn't shake the idea, *We die alone.* It had no simile. It had only closure. "Honey, you're exhausted," Eva answered me the night I called to tell her so after Charlie's two o'clock feeding, "it'll pass." "Postpartum depression." My mother shook her head. "Don't dwell, darling."

"It's not morbid," I insisted to Charlie over the next weeks. "It's not, truly. Facts can't be morbid. They're just facts." "What about Heaven?" Charlie knew by now to ask the right questions. We were lying in bed. We'd just made love and lay apart a little, holding hands. "What about the afterlife?" Charlie had been raised an Episcopalian, but religion was remote to him, impractical, and there was no passion in his tone. It was one of the reasons I loved him. He possessed morals and a benevolent spirit, but they had nothing to do with religion. "I don't think there is one," I said gravely. "So what is there?" Charlie rolled over on to me again. I could tell he wasn't taking the discussion seriously, but he played along to subvert trouble. "There's this," he answered himself as he took my hand and put it down on him. "I'm trying to make a point," I said, wounded. Charlie laughed at the pun. "Let's wake the baby up and play with him," he said.

But there was no getting around it for me, *We die alone,* and I looked into taking a course in Transcendental Meditation. A friend of mine in the Art Department had told me about it. He'd been through the class, and one day, as we'd sat in front of our easels painting from a model—the first nude male I'd ever contended with—he'd explained to me the Maharishi Mahesh Yogi's principles. "You meditate twice a day," he said. "Every day, twice a day for seven years. Then you get cosmic consciousness." "You get what?" "Cosmic consciousness." "What's that?— How come," I interjected, "male models wear underwear and female models don't?" "It's a law or something. I'm not sure what cosmic consciousness is. Our guide described it as *a sense of knowing.*" "Knowing what?" "My paintings of people always look too old," he answered. "I don't understand it. I paint what I see." "You're using too much color in the face, too many lines and shadows," I said. "It's tempting, but you've got to resist. You have to leave out most of what you see." "Heavy," my friend considered. "But how do you meditate?" I asked. "Just how do you do it?" "It's a secret." My friend soaked his rag in turpentine and wiped out the face on the canvas. "I'm afraid I'm bound to silence. I took a vow. Otherwise"—he began on his canvas with a clean, dry rag—"how'd they make any money?" "How much is it?" "Forty-five bucks, but if I recommend you, thirty." "Recommend me," I said. "I'd like to try it."

"I'm pleased," began the instructor a few nights later, "to see so many of you here." The instructor of meditation didn't look like I'd expected. He wore a business suit and his hair was cut short like a Rotcy's. But he had an accent that gave him away as a New Englander. In the middle of Missouri in the middle of winter, it lent him some authority. He'd traveled a long way to spread the word. I looked around the room as he spoke. Most of the students looked like me, scruffy, in torn jeans, lots of East Indian print shirts and blouses, dark sweaters, the odor of musk and sandalwood clinging to the fabrics. The men wore long hair. On the front row of the university classroom, however, sat a middle-aged couple, so conventionally dressed that anywhere else—on the streets of downtown Columbia, or in church—they wouldn't have been noticed. The woman, especially, worried me. She looked like one of my father's patients, someone who was coming to terms with bad news.

"It's like the surfaces of a deep pond," the instructor had

begun, drawing illustrations of the mind on the board. "Most of our thoughts are like waterwalkers skimming across. Meditation is like a pebble dropped into the center. It drifts down and down, down through the light shafts . . ." He began rhythmically sketching the pendulum progress of a stone. The crowd swayed a little. "Ya," breathed a student in front of me. I suspected he was stoned. The couple took each other's hands, like skaters. ". . . down into the dark sediment . . ." He stepped away from his drawing and nearly whispered, ". . . to rest on the bottom." I tried to concentrate on what the instructor was saying, but I couldn't take my eyes off the couple. Every word the instructor uttered looked to be of vital importance to them. I studied the woman's drawn face, her lace-collared dress, her shoes.

Now I saw that between the two of them, hers were the issues that had brought them here. The man was a support, a scaffolding. I could tell by the way he turned to her each time the instructor said something the man thought pertinent. The woman would squeeze his arm and nod. The instructor was drawing a sketch of the nervous system on the board, wiry lines inside a torso, then the head turned sideways, eyeless. His incorrect mappings of the nervous system irritated me. According to his figure we were wired like lamps. Along his wiring he drew little arrows, like twigs off a tree limb. "Of stress," he cooed, "thousands of barbs imbedding themselves as the days pass, the nights, the weeks, the years . . . Sometimes we explode in anger and can't explain it. Sometimes we get sick . . ." The woman's eyes filled with tears. She looked down quickly. Her husband leaned up on his chair and produced a handkerchief from his back pocket. It occurred to me that the woman was dying.

Before my initiation, which was to take place in a motor

146

lodge on the outskirts of Columbia, my friend from the Art Department sat with me in a sort of way station, a holding room from which we were to be called, one by one, and taken through the ritual. "No smoking," he said when I took out a cigarette. "Why not?" "No drugs, no stimulants of any kind. Just meditation." "Will meditating actually make me not want to smoke?" "So they say." My friend smiled dreamily. "Look around you." I glanced around the crowded office at the recent initiates and their sponsors, and at the people like me, still waiting, those who held a flower and a piece of fruit, items we'd been asked to bring. True enough that the veterans seemed calm. They lounged on the couches, caught the eyes of the initiates, and nodded. "You sure they're not on drugs?" I whispered to my friend. "Not even a little bit of grass?" "You'll see." He feigned a slow pose. I looked around for the couple. "Your turn." My friend took my arm as a man in a toga appeared at the door.

Meditation did not make me want to quit smoking. "It's because you left in the middle." My friend, disgusted, moved his easel across the studio from me a few days later. "It was stupid," I defended myself. "What was with the flowers, the fruit? What good did it do to offer them to an eight-by-ten glossy of a holy man in a cheap hotel room in the middle of Missouri? That grin, for God's sake. I was supposed to go down on my knees in front of *that* while a guy in a sheet babbled?" "That was Sanskrit." "No it wasn't." "Suit yourself," he said.

But in fact, I'd been afraid. As I'd walked through the ceremony with the guide, I couldn't help witnessing the whole thing through what I imagined to be the eyes of a dying woman, in her woman's dress, her husband at her arm, while the guide drew the shades and lit incense on the bureau. She seemed to be the composite of all the women at the clinic I'd ever watched enter the back rooms, take off their clothes, endure the exams, the biopsies, the surgeries, and die; women who, as wives and mothers through the fifties and sixties—represented in house-dresses and aprons in magazines, TV commercials—church-going, law-abiding women, I was supposed to take as my models. After all, wasn't I now a wife and mother? What exactly did that mean in 1971? *Passive, man*, Ray would have helped me out. Surely, then, the woman couldn't fall for it. Surely she couldn't believe, beyond the double bed with its chenille spread that smelled faintly of mildew and sex, in *cosmic consciousness*. Nor, in context, could I.

My guide had fallen, mumbling, to his knees in front of the photograph of the Maharishi. "Booga-booga," he might have said as he offered it the puny apple I'd bought at the all-night grocery, the carnation I'd borrowed from one of the other in-itiates. When I hadn't followed suit, he'd looked up at me im-patiently. "You're supposed to kneel," he said like an actor breaking character to complain about his costar. "I can't," I said. "Can I just stand?" "No," he grumbled. I could see his tennis shoes under his robe. "It's my background, I guess," I tried to explain, "you know, my religion. Southern Baptist via Dutch Reformist. 'Thou shalt have no other gods,' you know? Sorry," I added. He looked at me as though I were a leper. "Can't you just show me how to meditate?" I asked. "Just give me my mantra?" "It's supposed to come to me," he barked. He was still on the floor. "I mean," he tried to regain his composure, "while we're kneeling. It's like a gift, see, an awareness, and then I whisper it to you."

"Well, I just can't kneel," I said, "not in front of that picture. It's what you might call *a brazen image*." "OK, OK," my guide

148

said flatly. "Let me think a minute." He pulled himself up on the dresser and put his head in his hands. I could hear the trucks rumbling by on the interstate. Too quickly he looked up. "I-ing-a," he said. "What?" "I-ing-a. That's your mantra." "How'd you figure it?" "I told you, they come to me. Listen." The guide stood up and looked at his watch. "This just isn't for you." He rested his hand on my shoulder. "You're right," I said. "I'm sorry." After a moment I added, "You can keep the money, though. I did attend the classes . . ." "Can I keep the fruit, too?" he asked. "Sure," I said. "And the flower?" "Sure." "Sometimes people forget." "I see," I said. "Well, I'll walk you back," he said. "No, no," I said, "my car's just outside." I followed the sidewalk along the row of identical rooms facing the highway. Inside there was the same mumbling and I realized that there was a sort of assembly line initiation going on. I hurried by the office where my friend sat waiting for me, started the car, and drove out of the parking lot. As I turned the corner, I saw the couple. They were trying to cross the highway. They looked younger than I'd remembered, as earnest, a little shabby. The woman held her husband's arm as she peered around him. It had snowed the day before but now the sun was out. She looked perfectly healthy. She jumped back, laughing, to avoid being sprayed by a passing car.

CHAPTER *18* *THE CLASS OF 7308*

The Officers' Wives Orientation began with a film that was supposed to show us the future. A group of women in dresses and hats and white gloves were being taken, one by one, into the cockpit of a T-38. They looked silly in those clothes as they climbed up the little ladder, careful not to let their dresses fly up in the face of the colonel, right behind them. "Look at all them dials!" a particularly overdressed wife said to the colonel as he handed her the oxygen mask. The other women laughed on cue. In the next frame they were at a picnic. "He just won't talk to me," a woman in a red, white, and blue sailor blouse was saying to another. She reminded me of the models in the sportswear section of *The Seventeen Guide to Etiquette*. I looked down at my jeans, and around me in the half dark to the other wives in Indian skirts and tank tops. "Remember what the colonel's wife said," returned the friend on screen. "The boys are under a lot of pressure." For some reason, in the Air Force, people called one another "boys," or "girls," as if we existed in an arrested childhood. "There's a war to be fought. This year we girls must give one hundred percent to our marriages." The actress leaned down, and placing her hand on her friend's arm, looked meaningfully into her eyes.

Charlie, the baby, and I had arrived in Lubbock, Texas, a week before. We'd stayed in the Howard Johnson's until we'd found an apartment in Alpine Village, a row of ski lodge–type structures—ridiculous in the context of West Texas—across the alley from the only green expanse for miles, the Lubbock cemetery. Lubbock was called the Hub City, which meant that for miles in every direction there was nothing. Lubbock organized the nothing like the center of a wheel. As you approached from the desert southwest of Amarillo, grain refineries grew up on the horizon and the burn-off towers by the oil rigs were like great torches, the flames, as you came nearer, three and four stories high. Neither Charlie nor I had ever lived outside of Missouri. West Texas, with its flat red earth and huge sky, looked to us like the moonscapes the astronauts sent back from orbit. Years after we'd moved from there, I still found that dust in my dresser drawers, in the spines of my books, in shoes. There were days when the wind blew so hard across the plains that the sky turned dark, though the sun was shining, and you couldn't go out or you'd be blind awhile, your eyes stinging from the grit.

Lubbock was famous for tornadoes. The town itself had been devastated by one a few years back so that most of the buildings were new and they gave the place a futuristic quality, the one-way glass on the few skyscrapers mirroring clouds passing, like a video of the sky. Sometimes the baby and I drove out to the base and parked near the end of the runway so that we could watch the T-38s—beautiful little white jets which seated the pilot and instructor one behind the other—take off at the opposite end. The heat drifted up off the runways like a mirage, and when the pilot lit his afterburners, the plane nearly disappeared in a liquid haze before it catapulted into the sky.

T-38s were the last in the series of planes students would fly before they graduated from pilot training and began serving their six years in the Air Force. The class started in T-41s, little Cessnas like the ones Charlie and I had flown together in Missouri. Then they moved on to the T-37, what the instructors called "the world's biggest dog whistle," because of the noise it made. If you were going to wash out—fail pilot training— most likely you'd fail in the T-37. To begin with, it was hard for students to make the transition into jets, and the T-37 was difficult to fly. Many of the pilots couldn't get over the airsickness. It looked like Charlie might be one of them.

During his first weeks in the T-37, he'd come home pale, weak in the knees. Already several of his classmates had dropped out and headed, most of them, for navigator school. "Look," I advised him, "just take Dramamine for a few flights. Maybe you'll get over it." "I can't." Charlie sat down on the couch and put his head between his legs. "They do urine tests every few days on some of us. They look for drugs. I could be thrown out on that alone." "Do you know who'll be tested?" "It's random. It could be anyone." Charlie moaned. "I'm such a weak puke." "A what?" "A weak puke." He grinned. "That's what they call the guys who barf in the cockpit." "But aren't they looking for marijuana?" "Does it make a difference?" "I don't know," I said, "I'll call Dad and ask him."

My mother answered the phone. "Debbie, *dar*ling," she sang when she heard my voice, "how are you? How's our baby?" "Fine, Mom, listen, I've got a question for you. Could you detect Dramamine in someone's urine? I mean, if you were testing urine for drugs, would Dramamine show up?" "Poor *Char*lie." My mother understood immediately. "Just a moment, dear, I'll get your father." How my parents loved Charlie. "Deb?" I heard my father on the line. There was humor and affection in his voice. He liked to be called on medical matters. Growing up, none of us had had a doctor other than our father. He'd given us all our shots, taken care of us when we were sick. I'd never had a physical exam until I was pregnant. Now he was more than willing to be Charlie's doctor, too.

"Dad says he doesn't think so," I told Charlie when I hung up the phone. "He says if he were you he'd take a chance. And he says airsickness is a little like morning sickness. It passes." "That sounds like your dad." Charlie shook his head as he put the baby in the car, but I could tell he was comforted. Charlie and I cruised the streets around the university, then headed toward Lubbock's downtown. Since we did all of our shopping at the base, the city was unfamiliar, with its neighborhoods of squat stucco houses, the expanses of rubble bordering the new shopping malls. When we found an all-night drugstore on the outskirts of Lubbock, just to be safe, I went in to buy the Dramamine while Charlie kept the engine running. "I got it!" I said as I climbed back into the car. "Did you see anyone?" Charlie asked. "Anyone from the base?" "No. No one. Now listen, Dad said take one right now"—I offered Charlie the foil-covered sheet of yellow pills—"and one in the morning. They make you tired, so drink a lot of coffee, and eat bread, a roll or something. Don't go up on an empty stomach."

When Charlie got home the next evening, I was waiting for him in a lounge chair in the carport. The baby dozed in his playpen. We'd been over at the cemetery most of the afternoon. "Grass," I'd say to the baby, "real grass, honey." "Geen," he'd answered me as he pulled himself up on a headstone. "How did it go?" I greeted Charlie. "OK," he said, amazed. "I did it. I flew that sucker, and I didn't barf, didn't even feel like I was going to . . ." "Did they test anybody?" "Ya, but not me." He grinned as he moved toward the playpen. "Let's wake him up

and play with him," he said. "Go ahead," I said. "Now," Charlie
spoke softly into the baby's ear, "if I can just get through the
next week or so . . ."

We'd begun pilot training in May of 1972, an election year.
For Charlie and me, it was the first election in which we could
vote. I'd turned twenty-two in February and Charlie was
twenty-three. We voted absentee, Charlie for Nixon, I for
McGovern. Maybe it made up for my having campaigned, in
fifth grade—to my parents' delight—for Nixon. People often
said about Charlie and me that we seemed ill-matched. What
they meant was that Charlie looked like a citizen and I "like,
like . . ." They couldn't find a word for me. "Hippie" served
the less imaginative ones. Charlie liked the sound of these comments. He'd laugh about them in bed, mimic the voices, then
hold me. In the end I think he believed he'd saved me from
some things—from the public humiliation of having flunked
out of school, from people like Ray.

He'd been the one to encourage me, after the baby was born,
to reapply to schools in Columbia. "You had a bad year," he'd
insist. "It happens to a lot of people. Just explain it to them."
"Easy for you to say," I'd argue. "No one will have me now."
But I did reapply to several schools. Charlie went with me to
the interviews. The university and another school refused me
flat out. But the third, a small liberal arts school that had just
gone coed, bent the rules for me. Charlie and I had sat in the
president's office and explained my situation. At the end of my
story, the president sat back. "Well," he answered, "fair enough.
Now if I understand you, you're asking for another chance."
"Yes." I sat up earnestly. "We'll take you on probation," he'd
responded. Tears filled Charlie's eyes. "See?" he said to me in
the car. "People are basically good, you know?"

Once, during our last year in Missouri—I'd been admitted to the university by then—when the division between the Rotcies and the war protesters was at its greatest, when even the professors sneered at the students in uniform, I'd come down, during my poetry class, with some bug that made me suddenly faint. I'd left class early, but as I cleared the steps outside the Arts and Science Building, I collapsed in the grass among students who looked like me, students wearing torn jeans and Mexican ponchos, bandannas, no shoes. I lay on the grass awhile, then tried to get up again only to reel and fall. People thought, no doubt, I was on drugs. Some turned, smiling, to watch me. "Come here," I asked anyone. "I'm sick or something."

Finally I crawled over to the sidewalk. A boy in a Rotcy uniform was about to pass. "Listen," I said, grabbing his leg. He stopped short. "My husband is Charlie Digges," I said. "You know him?" "No he's not," the Rotcy answered. "He is," I said. "I'm supposed to meet him in front of the Art Department, but I'm sick or something. I can't walk. Would you go get him? Would you tell him I'm over here, please?" "OK, OK." He'd backed off. By now the people on the lawn behind me began jeering him. Someone threw a candy wrapper. I knew he'd agreed just to get away. I lay back on the grass and I must have passed out, because the next thing I knew, Charlie was carrying me to the car. He'd waded through the group, in full uniform, and picked me up. Charlie wasn't much taller than me, but he carried me lightly, holding my head against his shoulder.

In late October, just before the election, Nixon called off the war. Many of the student pilots were devastated by the news. It meant, among other things, that war or not, they'd just signed on to six years in the Air Force. For the diehards—those who would have joined the Air Force anyway—it meant that there would be fewer F-4s offered at graduation. F-4s were fighter jets, sleek, dark planes that flew combat missions over Southeast Asia. The best pilots in any class always chose the F-4s. At the weekend parties various members of the class threw, one of the instructors might produce a recording of a real F-4 combat mission, and all the men would stop what they were doing and crowd around the tape player.

Since I was uncomfortable with the wives—they seemed more and more to me like grown-up versions of the experts from my Home Economics class years ago—I stayed close to Charlie at all the parties, and I'd find myself among the students as they listened to the pilots on tape go through their checklists, joke with one another, plane to plane, over the radio while they waited to get clearance for takeoff. An F-4 mission involved at least four planes, with a pilot and navigator in each cockpit, one behind the other. They flew in close formation toward the target. You could hear behind the roar of the engines and the static the garbled voice of the leadman as he evaluated the approach or gave instructions to his wingmen. Sometimes they encountered enemy fighters and dogfought at thirty thousand feet. Sometimes the formation lost a plane.

All of it, beginning to end, was on the tape. "I'm hit, I'm hit. Fuck a duck. Going down," one of the wingmen shouted. "Punch out! Punch out!" the pilots spoke at once. "Listen to this," the instructor manning the recorder would grin as he rewound the tape and turned the volume up high. "I love you, Mom," you could barely hear above the roar. "I love you, Mom!" one of the students would shriek as the group broke up laughing. It was a standard phrase for pilots. It ended, we would come to find out, most black-box cockpit recordings, whether military or otherwise, when the flight ended in disaster. Like "shit-hot," and "jet jockey," "good hands," "that really blows your skirt up," "pud knocker," "don't go inverted," "weak puke," and many others, it was part of an insiders' language Charlie's class was learning, day by day. There was fear in the students' laughter following each tape those evenings, and after the cease-fire in 1972, there was also a bitterness, like envy.

An F-4 pilot who'd been an instructor at Reese, Charlie's training base just outside of Lubbock, had gone down a year or so before in the South China Sea. His wingmen thought he had survived the explosions. After he'd ejected, they said, they'd watched as a Viet Cong patrol had picked him up out of the water. He'd been listed M.I.A. His wife and children lived on the base. At any military installation across the country or abroad, you could buy copper bracelets which had etched across them the names of the men in the Army, Air Force, Navy, or Marines who were either missing in action or prisoners of war. The point was to wear the bracelet until those men made it home. Everyone at Reese, including Charlie and me, wore the F-4 M.I.A.'s bracelet.

After the election of 1972, the planeloads of P.O.W.'s and M.I.A.'s arrived on the West Coast. They'd wander across the tarmac and into the lens of the TV cameras. They looked thin and confused. Their grinning seemed otherworldly, their reunions with their families, panicked. Word had spread across the base that the M.I.A. whose bracelet we all wore had come back on one of the flights. The story was he'd been in a P.O.W. camp for the past year and that he was forgoing, at least for now, traveling to one of the rehabilitation sites the government had set up around the country. No one had seen him since he'd been back. "Those are 141s." Charlie pointed out the cargo jets from which the men on TV unloaded. "They're your ticket to the airlines."

It was still weeks to graduation, but the list of planes to be offered to the Class of 7308 was on everyone's mind, the pilots and their wives. The kind of plane each student chose determined where he'd train, and where, for the next few years, his family would be stationed. Remote tours were still a possibility. Based on the planes they chose, pilots might be sent to the various outposts in Asia. In those cases, families wouldn't be allowed to accompany them. As they entered their last weeks of training, the competition between the men turned fierce. The academic part of the program had concluded. Charlie finished with excellent scores. He must fly, now, daily, in perfect formation in the T-38s, every detail of his training mission, from split-second timing to his efficient execution of acrobatic maneuvers—aileron rolls and Cuban eights—recorded and evaluated.

Who finished first would have first pick of the planes. Who finished second, would have second pick, and so on. By March of 1973, with less than a month to go, the top five scores, Charlie's among them, fluctuated daily by fractions of a point. The original class of fifty-seven students had shrunk to thirty-eight. Then, with only two weeks to go, the list of planes was posted. It included three F-4s, one a reconnaissance plane—"a picture taker," as Charlie called it—a DC-9, some OV-10s, C-130s, KC-135s, B-52s, an A-7, some instructor slots, and two 141s—huge jet cargo planes like the ones that had carried the P.O.W.'s home, one to fly out of New Jersey, the other to fly out of Southern California in what was called the Pacific system. In the end, Charlie chose the 141 to California.

"You guys will never know what it was like," the officer's voice shook. He was sweating, and he used the back of his hand to wipe his forehead, then brought his fist down on the podium, harder, it seemed, than he'd meant to. He stared at his hand a moment as some of the pages from his speech skidded onto the floor. He let them lie there. He'd long since abandoned the polite, patriotic rhetoric with which he'd begun his address to the Class of 7308 on the occasion of their graduation. The base chapel was crowded—the pilots, in their dress uniforms, occupying the first three rows, and behind them their families. Charlie's and my family had made the trip to Texas to see him graduate. My sisters Connie and Beth had come, and my younger brothers, David and Stevie.

For the last hour, the officer—the F-4 pilot who'd been listed missing in action and who'd come back, miraculously, on one of the planes in January, the officer whose bracelet, even as he spoke, we wore—had described, in detail, the mission which had ended in his capture by the Viet Cong. Most of us knew the story. He and his wingmen had been on their way to a target, supposedly an ammunition site near the Cambodian border. They'd run into a fleet of Russian MiGs. When he'd been hit from behind he'd punched out over the South China Sea. At first the officer's diversion from his text seemed planned, the way ministers dramatically interrupt themselves to illustrate a point. Halfway through his narrative, it was clear that the pilot had not only told this story many, many times, but that he was compelled to recount it again.

It was as if the audience didn't matter, as if the reason he told it had to do with the fact that it had never, to his way of thinking, come out right. He had it down to a clean cause-effect, his diction typically military, full of the jargon with which we'd all become familiar over the past nine months, a jargon that undercut his terror, objectified the enemy. "Well, here come the gooks out of the sun, boys. I said, OK, OK . . . I was talking to number three . . . I think it was number three . . ." The way the officer culled details, hesitated, repeated words, suggested that the story contained a secret not yet revealed to him. "What

159

could they do?" He referred to his wingmen who had circled him, protected him as long as they could before their low fuel sent them back. "What could they do?" he said over and over, his voice turning cynical, then pleading, as if tone, itself, might crack the case. Voice lowered, he backed away from the story. Leaning forward, he seemed to be trying to sneak up on it, as if to catch it unaware.

"Well," he said after a moment. He looked defeated, tired. He put his hand to his forehead again and began massaging his temples. "So here they come now in their little boat . . ." The flight instructors and the base commander who sat behind him on the stage stirred uneasily in their chairs. The general looked at his watch and nodded to something an instructor whispered. It seemed that the officer was about to begin on his twelve months in a prisoner-of-war camp, and that would never do, not here, in front of wives and parents, not the isolation box in which prisoners were made to crouch for days at a time, not the interrogation sessions, the beatings. You could see it on the general's face as he weighed possible strategies to interrupt the officer without embarrassing everyone. Probably he knew the details, had heard them in the Officers' Club bar, or in the debriefing rooms. A baby began to cry in the middle rows of the chapel, and as the mother, holding the child, made her way out, the general and the instructors used the distraction simply to begin applauding. The pilots caught on, and the audience. The officer, confused, lowered his head and pushed himself off from the podium like a swimmer from the edge of a pool. We stood applauding as he was ushered out of the chapel.

CHAPTER *19* TOMBS OF THE MUSES

It was in Lubbock, Texas, during Charlie's pilot training that I began to write poetry. I began to write in answer to an essay I read one winter morning before dawn while a terrific dust storm blew outside, the sudden gusts shouldering our windows. I had no idea that that essay had already been answered many times. The baby lay with me on the couch. We'd been up most of the night. He was running a fever and we were waiting for it to be seven o'clock so that I could call the base doctor and make an appointment to take him in. Charlie had left before five. Storm or not, his class met every day. Maybe they'd study charts and systems or fly the simulators. Or maybe by afternoon the winds would die down and they would take up their planes. At any rate we wouldn't see him until late that evening.

Little Charlie lay across my lap with a washcloth over his forehead. He'd finally fallen asleep. The brilliant, high color in his cheeks softened, and I could feel, where his head rested against my thigh, that his fever had subsided. We'd had many such nights and mornings since moving to Texas. All fall and winter, no doubt because of the dust, the baby had trouble with croup. In the beginning his barking cough, followed by a high fever, had filled me with panic. By the doctors' direction I'd built over his bed a croup tent, a sheet nailed to his wall that draped over the crib, and over a humidifier. The croup tent scared the baby and so I always climbed in with him. I'd bring a flashlight and a paper cup—tiny holes pricked in its base— remembering, from Sunday school, a little trick which had fascinated me. We shone the light under the cup and the ceiling of our tent filled with foggy stars. Then I'd read *Good Night Moon*, over and over, until the baby fell asleep.

Still, I was afraid to leave him; his coughing often awakened him, and after a while I thought to bring my own books under the tent. As he slept I read Dickinson, Whitman—and on that particular winter dawn, after we had moved out to the living room couch—Emerson. I still have those books whose pages are forever swollen from the humidifier's steam, some of them with a trace of red dust in the bindings. In the essay I read that morning, Emerson described the character of a poet and the conditions of his art.

. . . the poet turns the world to glass, and shows us all things in their right series and procession . . . This is true science. The poet alone knows astronomy, chemistry, vegetation, and animation, for he does not stop at these facts, but employs them as signs. He knows why the plain, or meadow of space, was strewn with these flowers we call suns and moons and stars . . .

That Emerson addressed the poet as "he" bothered me not at all. I have always read myself relentlessly and without reproach into the masculine, perhaps because as a child I'd believed myself to be, somehow, a boy, a boy arrested at adolescence. That I became a woman seemed simply an imposition of the body onto the mind, and in the end, I celebrated the complication. It made for the continuous cultivation of a secret life and a sense of a peculiar anonymity which, in the long run, I have come to understand as the source of my writing. Even now it seems right that at the onset of their own adolescence—at twelve or thirteen—my sons and I have worn clothing of the same size. At their puberties, their hands and feet have measured precisely the same as mine. And as we have charted on our various kitchen door frames across the country the points at which they have outgrown me, I have had the feeling that I've sent them ahead as men, while at five feet five inches, I remain the boy, and the woman, who gave birth to them.

Nothing in my background said I could, or even should, attempt this thing so foreign to me, the poem. I had never formally studied writing of any kind. All through high school I'd taken science courses. I'd never made better than C's in composition classes. I knew my written grammar was poor and that I couldn't spell. But over the next weeks and months in Texas, as I wrote down lines on a legal pad, wrote sometimes under the croup tent, the humidifier whirring, the paper, pen, my hair, everything slowly soaking through until the ink began to bleed, the issues of proper syntax and grammar seemed, for the moment, · unimportant; as unimportant, for instance, as the fact that year after year, unable to find a screwdriver, my father had secured the fifty or more storm windows on the house in Missouri with a kitchen knife. . . . *workmen, work, and tools, words and things, birth and death . . . The poet . . . gives them a power which makes their old use forgotten . . .*

And no doubt, with my head full of Yeats or Eliot or Thomas, there was something about the West Texas landscape that demanded I answer it, as well as Emerson, during those early morning drives to the base hospital, or in the afternoons, to the end of the runway, where I'd stop the car and take the baby on my lap so that he, too, could see the planes taking off and landing. *The path of things is silent. Will they suffer a speaker to go with them?* One day all the wives and children of the pilots were invited to come out to a field to watch the men practice parachuting. Five or six at a time, they were tethered by ropes to the backs of trucks, and with the bright orange silk billowing out behind them, the men, running twenty yards or so, appeared suddenly to levitate into the air. Cut free, carried awhile by the winds, some of them drifted so far west, the sun erased them. In Texas, so much looking into the sky! Nothing stopped the mind from wandering. Sun-blinded, your eyes teared. *A very high sort of seeing . . .* When you rubbed them, you saw stars.

Maybe I began to write poetry in answer to the confused politics of that time. We were nobody—Charlie, the baby, and me—to the huge military construct that had brought us to Texas. We had been spun out, like so many others, onto the American landscape, as if by some great destiny machine. Everything about our lives that year—from the empty tundra to the tract house we lived in, to the uniforms the pilots wore, and in their way, the uniforms of the wives—sought to efface us. *How cheap even the liberty then seems . . . Dream delivers us to dream.* And yet, as the sixth of ten children, I suppose I meant to challenge that effacement. I'd spent, by then, twenty-two years learning how to make myself heard. What better way than to adopt a medium as silent, as cold, and as abstract as language? "Hair of the dog," as my father might have said. *The soul makes the body . . .*

You might say I'd had a very long childhood, a childhood I couldn't help but confuse with my brothers' and sisters'. Even now, whether I look ahead of me to Eva, Gena, Rena, Paul, and Everett, or behind me to Connie, David, Beth, and Steve, it is sometimes hard to distinguish what happened to whom, and when. Was it my doll or Connie's—named Meg, or Amy —which I found in the orchard only a year ago, rotted, all but her beautiful wooden head? *But the quality of the imagination is to flow, and not to freeze.* Was it my crime or Eva's that saw me running one March afternoon to the pond, climbing inside a huge erosion rut, crying myself to sleep? Why were the banks so steep that spring? What year was it? Who found me? Or did I simply wake in the dark and walk home? It seemed vital to me that someone answer these questions, or invent the answers the way my mother did on each of our ten birthdays when she passed around the dinner table the same dog-eared snapshot of an infant lying peacefully on her and my father's bed. "That's you." She'd smile at the birthday boy or girl. "I'm quite sure now that it's you. I remember precisely the moment your father took it. It was a beautiful January/ February/ March/ May/ June/ July/ August/ September/ November morning . . ."

Those probably weren't poems I wrote in Texas. None, thankfully, have survived the eleven moves I've made around the country since 1973. People have suggested to me that I should have saved them, that someday I'll be sorry I threw them, city by city, away. I don't think so. Even now I throw out so much. I'm never sure if what I write is worth saving. Moreover, I think I write to be saved; from what, I'm not sure, since salvation comes always with the next poem, the one I'm about to write. The point is that in Texas I believed that they were, or could be, poems, the way I'd once believed in prayer. When the baby was born, I'd given up Christianity, but I would always be religious. Writing became my religion. Images from the Scriptures, the settings and details from the many Bible stories I knew, scientific data, memories of the orchard, the lab, the pond, along with all those years of looking, painting what I saw, began a strange metamorphosis—*On the brink of the waters of life and truth, we are miserably dying*—because I was alone for the first time. And I could look out that window, morning or evening, and see nothing at all.

CHAPTER *20* *THE THREE-*
THOUSAND-
HOUR CLUB

When we arrived in California in August of 1973, the revolution—whatever it had been, whatever we'd imagined it to be—was over. We drove in from the Mohave toward the foothills of San Bernardino, drove over the bald brown tundra that met a gray horizon where, as Charlie pointed out, "There are supposed to be mountains," and it was as if we'd entered the purely present tense, that youngest edge of the continent where everything—the weather, political movements, fads—originated, and since this was so, was not in the least concerned with history. History began here, and history, like an engine, had no memory, no notion of chronology. This was why, as the realtors confirmed during the next several weeks, you could drive some winter morning up to Big Bear and ski, ice-skate, drive back down onto the plain that afternoon and sunbathe, watch the hummingbirds at the feeders. Why, after the Santa Ana winds that each October swept the smog out over the Pacific, the mountains suddenly appeared. Then you'd lose your sense of direction, pull into the wrong carport, so disorienting was this new view and the smell of orange blossoms. The lights below the timberline might be confused with stars.

There was no trace, as far as we could tell, of the political troubles so publicized in California during the sixties. The P.O.W.'s and M.I.A.'s, landing at the various Army and Air Force bases along the coast, had long since greeted their families to cameras flashing behind the chain-link fences; had accepted, in mass ceremonies, their flying crosses and Purple Hearts; endured the trips home and the hometown demonstrations; and disappeared. Now the runways at Norton, which was to be our base, looked deserted. The huge bay doors of the 141s gaped open, though their cockpits glowed green against the evening sky.

In Southern California there was one season, the realtor told us as we rode around San Bernardino in her Lincoln, but it had many names—fire season, the rainy season, the smog alerts. As for the San Andreas fault, visible along the northwest shelf between the mountains and the valley, "No one," she told us, "pays much attention. Listen"—she touched Charlie's knee— "a little rumble now and then, no more. You're smarter to buy flood insurance, for God's sake." We passed the junk shops along Waterman Avenue in which figurines of Elvis and pink madonnas sat atop stained canvas trunks brought out on the wagon trains. The brass labels on the flattops, as I would discover later, chronicled our own journey—*S. Gear, St. Joseph, Missouri, A. E. Meek and Co., Denver, Colorado*. The ribs of Conestogas were wound with Christmas lights and they framed displays of geodes, yellowed christening gowns, fool's gold, seashells found on the tops of mountains, paintings on black velvet of *The Last Supper*, matadors, Santa Claus on a surfboard.

What had been a mission was now a furniture outlet, the multicolored crushed velvet couches spilling out of the sanctuary under the empty bell tower, the bell, in fact, for sale, and the huge cypress-wood cross. During the rainy season, she explained, as we headed up into the hills, houses might be washed down the mountainside, but construction began again, when things dried up, on the same sandy shelves, "and the property values double." She stopped the car at the overlook and pressed the automatic windows. The heat blast caught in our throats. "See?" she said. "Everyone has a pool." She swept her hand across the view, across the hundreds of bright bodies of water, round and square and kidney-shaped, some with beer signs painted on the bottom, or tropical fish, or the American flag. They organized the basin like so many clear consciences.

We'd been in our new condominium a week when Charlie received his first orders to fly, with his crew, to the Azores. There he waited nearly five weeks on one of the islands, pending possible trouble in the Middle East. Little Charlie and I waited where the months' accumulated heat hollowed out the valley and crept up the mountains. By now the foothills were a deep brown and the field behind us seemed to dissolve beyond our wall. All day and evening the 141s cleared the runways and headed west over the Pacific, cleared our little village that sat on the east edge of San Bernardino in the suburb of Highland. Many Air Force families lived in Pinehurst Village. You knew the senior pilots' residences by the Corvettes in their carports. It had seemed like a good idea for us to buy a condominium in Pinehurst Village. We'd never owned a home, but the V.A. allowed us to put only five hundred dollars down, and the monthly payments were cheap, less than the rent we'd paid in Texas. The base itself was a mile away and so we were close to the commissary, the base doctors. Little Charlie, who'd turned three in May, had the company of other pilots' children. In the afternoons at the pool or the playground he and his friends, each time a plane passed over, would point to the sky and say "Daddy."

I hoped to make friends with the other wives, but that proved difficult. In order for the women to make friends, our husbands needed to fly the same missions, and that was rare. When the men, typically gone for two or three weeks at a stretch, came home, it was understood that no one was to bother that couple. You'd see them, a day or two after the man had arrived home, packing the car for a week at the beach or the mountains. Or they'd hole up in their condominium, their children wandering around the complex, dropping in to play whole afternoons and into the evenings. If your own husband was away, it was your job to entertain the children, feed them, even carry them, sleeping, home across the lawns, dodging the sprinkler systems as you went. Mostly, I came to identify the other women by whose mother they were. "You fed Jeanne twice last week," a woman introduced herself to me one afternoon. "Now you send Charlie over when your husband gets home."

In late September the fires began above Bluejay and in a few days' time, they'd climbed to the timberline, the valley surrounded by a smoke rain. As the baby and I drove in from the freeway between the acres of orange groves sentried along the road by huge palms, I felt an immoral thrill at the wall of black smoke through which sun-colored flames flickered. The fires produced a strange, elevated wind that blew the palm fronds wildly, scattering the husks, the size of men, across our path. Against the background of black mountains and sky, the desert, dotted with bright-colored stucco residences, looked like those landscapes set up on plywood through which a model train is driven.

I'd never live again where the particulars of place so quickly and efficiently obliterated the memory of others; live in such a way that what I'd been taught, what I believed, didn't seem to apply. While Charlie was away, the baby and I invented our days. I'd call the squadron to hear the same bored voice say, "He's still in the system. No firm ETA. Try tomorrow." Then what did we do? As the fires spread, the radio broadcasts warned us not to go out. The smog, trapped in the basin, and the smoke made the air outside dangerous to breathe. We might spend the morning, then, trying to lure the coyotes, driven down into the valley, into our tiny backyard. The animals were by now so starved they'd lost their fear and wandered, hollow-eyed, across the Pinehurst Village lawns. When I ran out of hamburger, I began cutting up sirloin steaks and let little Charlie toss the pieces, one by one, out our sliding glass door.

Sometimes we made calls to Missouri. It was autumn there. My mother would say how the leaves in the park across the street were changing, how my father had already had to cover the mums during an early cold spell. I'd stand at our back door that looked out over the field and beyond it the foothills, soot-clouded, the dark base of the mountains, and try to replace what I saw with what I remembered—the dense, intimate green of the Midwest, the tree-banked hills, the girders, as you crossed the bridge over the Missouri, blinking light and shadow as you made your way fast to the interstate, the way my mother's voice was swallowed, just then, by the roar of a plane taking off or landing. In that moment what she described came suddenly clear to me and I longed for home. I could place it like the smell of mothballs on all the coats of my childhood. When her voice found focus, I gave the receiver to her grandson.

Then the phone would ring some night late and the officer would report, "Your husband's crew's inbound. He'll be landing at 0300 hours." I'd get up and make coffee, take a bath and wash my hair, sit waiting until the baby woke at seven. We'd pass the morning running errands, shopping for groceries, taking care of any details that might take us away from Charlie once he arrived home. Sometimes we'd run into other women and their children. The ones whose carts were full like ours were getting ready for someone's arrival. They were animated, friendly. The women were dressed neatly and wore, like me, bright makeup, and the children's faces were clean. Those whose carts bore a few frozen dinners didn't expect their husbands home for a while. They maneuvered the aisles quickly, embarrassed to be seen in dirty jeans. When, by late afternoon, Charlie still hadn't arrived, I'd call the base. "Sorry," the voice would reply. "At the last minute they had to pick up a part at Hickam. I'd say they'll be in sometime tonight, but don't quote me."

Evenings, when the smog rose a little and it was slightly cooler, I liked to take the baby across the wall into a desert field that ran for several miles to the east of us toward the foothills. The field had been part of Norton Air Force Base during the Second World War and though all the Quonset huts had been dismantled, the concrete squares on which they'd been erected and the paths that had once led to the doors organized the area. You could tell where the windows had been by the few scrawny cacti and philodendron that grew halfway along the slabs. The yards—marked off by cinder block—had gone back to sand. A few huge, dead trees, eucalyptus or sycamore, said here was the entrance. Rarely did we see anyone else in the field, except in the spring when a mountain wash cutting through the sand to the south was filled and nearly rushed toward a viaduct positioned just beyond Pinehurst Village. What had looked to be dead brush along the wash came to life and a fissure of green spread up from the banks. The cacti, half a mile away, bloomed huge red flowers, and people from the area actually brought towels and umbrellas and lay out by the stream.

The field was an ideal place to wait while the planes took off or landed to the north, so close they passed over like huge, slow fish, and you could easily make out their call signs, glimpse the pilots in the cockpit when they turned west, the sun, before we were blinded, cutting them out in miniature, and you knew the immensity of the craft. C-141s are beautiful planes, smaller and more gracefully elongated than C-5s, whose fat underbellies parody huge pelicans. Norton's 141 fleet was white, the noses of the planes a black circle. Once I carted a deck chair over to the field, and, placing it at the center of one of the slabs, the baby and I sat counting the takeoffs and landings as a full moon rose over the mountains just as the sun was setting. For a few minutes, we centered the balance. We hid the chair in what looked to have been a dugout, and after that, brought over a Wiffle ball and bat. I'd pitch to little Charlie where we imagined the World War II pilots had played, though it was hard to tell where the diamond had been. Like the jungle, the desert erases everything inside of a few years. That's what I came to love about it. In this way our waiting turned into something else, into its own strange activity, like an obsession with imagining how you'd furnish empty rooms.

Then Charlie would walk in the door. He'd be laden with gifts, a pearl ring and jade earrings for me, wooden planes and trucks from the Philippines for the baby. One morning near three he and his crew pulled up in a pickup and unloaded stereo speakers, turntable, amplifier, a rattan, glass-top trunk, three wall clocks, and ten monkeywood salad sets, Christmas presents, explained Charlie, for my family. The men, slim and handsome, looked amazingly alike in their green flight suits, combat boots, their hair cut short, an identical sunburn delineating Air Force issue sunglasses across their faces, and they smelled, all of them, wonderfully of sweat and coffee and other countries. "Would you like something to drink?" I offered, glad I'd put on my prettiest robe, brushed my hair. The crew looked hard at me. "No thanks." Charlie's copilot smiled. "We still have three more stops to make." He stepped aside so that I could see, by the carport light, the pickup full of couches, Papa-San chairs, brass coat racks.

Charlie and I would sit up talking, making love until sunrise, arranging the new furniture, drinking coffee. Once, after a trip to New Zealand, we stayed up all night cleaning and defrosting the refrigerator to make room for the many boxes of crabmeat he and his crew had brought home. They'd kept the meat and the New Zealand butter cold by storing it, during the trip, in the wheel locks of the aircraft. Because he'd traveled through so many time zones, Charlie's days and nights would be confused; he told me how, often, when he took off to the west, he could actually see the sun rise twice in the same day. The 141s flew long legs over the Pacific. It was an eight-hour trip, for instance, to Hawaii, the point of departure for most of his missions. Sometimes he'd be twenty-four hours in daylight. Charlie owned a watch that kept the time of every country on earth, its series of rings punctuated with a tiny window in which the date changed, swept by a minute and a second hand. When he came home, he usually slept in while the baby and I went about our day, little Charlie playing quietly, with his new toys, around the bed.

About the time Charlie found our schedule again, new orders would come in and he'd be off to Asia, Europe, the Middle East. His missions usually consisted of transporting supplies from one military installation to another. In the wake of the war his squadron flew refugees out of Saigon. The last president of Vietnam was known to have immigrated to the U.S., escaping to California on a 141 in the early seventies. It was rumored he ran a liquor store in Orange County. As late as 1975 Norton crews flew what were called the baby lifts, during which war orphans, arriving at bases across the West Coast, were adopted by American families on the spot. At the end of our first year in California, we figured that Charlie had been away more than half of it, averaging two weeks a month in the system for twelve months. "If they keep this up"—he'd shake his head—"I'll soon be a member of the Three-Thousand-Hour Club." Charlie sat at the dining room table in his flight suit. He'd be leaving again in a few minutes. Say it was August again, or September, and the desert light flooded our rooms. The mountains, which had stunned us all winter, had disappeared, and the huge stones in the foreground that was the field looked like sheep grazing. On the left pocket of his flight suit, over his silver wings, Charlie wore a tiny pin that confirmed he'd already logged over one thousand hours in the air. He touched the pin and laughed weakly, trying to catch my eyes. He was compelled, more and more, to make the point that his absence wasn't his fault, or that this year's schedule looked to be lighter, or that maybe sometime I could go with him. He made such points often. After a year in California, things did not go well with us.

CHAPTER *21* *A MAN GOES*
TRAVELING,
A STRANGER
COMES TO TOWN

My brother told me a story in our parents'
kitchen about a year ago. It was Christmas Day and there was
an icy rain falling. It had fallen all night and was falling in the
afternoon as he told me the story. All the trees were slick with
it. Lucky there was no wind or whole boughs would have broken off. Or if the sun had shone the orchard would have looked
to be made of glass. Steve and I were having a cup of coffee.
There'd been trouble between us recently which the advent of
a story seemed to heal a little.

Just that past autumn, he began, someone rang our parents'
doorbell. "It was Andres Price," Steve said, "Andres Price, the
Haitian." Our father had spent some time in Haiti in 1964. Price
had been his assistant at the Albert Schweitzer Hospital in the
Artibonite Valley, not far from the capital. He'd taken it upon
himself to be our father's interpreter and friend.

Why had our father gone to Haiti? Steve and I didn't bother
to raise this question. Maybe there'd been a call for doctors—
he'd probably read about it somewhere. When we were children, during dinner prayers, there was a longing in our father's

voice as he asked God to watch over the missionaries "in the foreign fields," he'd say, a phrase I loved and listened for. On the shortwave radio next to his bed he'd tune in distant places. He could get Quito, Ecuador. Quito broadcast a religious program, the opening of which was a chorus singing "Jesus Saves," swallowed at intervals by static. "That's the ocean." Our father would wink at us and fiddle with the dials.

Steve remembered better than I what it had been like to have our father away. Had it been two weeks? "Over a month," Steve corrected me. "Don't you remember the cable? The letters? Haiti's not so far from here." Maybe our father had reassured him with these words years ago. As Steve told it, Price had emigrated from Haiti some years back. He'd ended up in New York City and he'd meant to come out to Missouri immediately, but he had no money. He'd worked in a liquor store on 42nd Street for the past fifteen years. During their time together at the Schweitzer Hospital our father had been impressed with Price's skills as a surgical assistant. Maybe he'd extended an invitation to Price to come to work for him in America. In 1964 the clinic was busy. Our father could barely handle all the patients. "Listen," Steve stopped me. I was running away with his story. "I doubt if Dad ever asked him to come. It was probably Price's idea."

But surely in Haiti our father had told Price about his plans for the clinic, how, one by one, his sons would come back to work with him there. In 1964 Everett was finishing up his surgical residency in Boston. Paul was in medical school. At the youngest end of the family there were David and Steve, who would come into the practice just when the older boys needed time off to travel, to do research. It would be quite a place, the clinic. Maybe they'd have to build a bigger one, clear the orchard and break ground. "Stop harping on that," Steve interrupted

me. "Price probably wasn't even formally trained. Where do
you get that information? Who said Dad ever asked him?" Still,
I imagined our father explaining the idea to Price as they
prepped for surgery or dressed a wound. He believed it. We all
believed it in 1964. Say Andres Price had listened and begun
making plans.

"What did Dad say to him that night?" I asked my brother.
"What did Andres Price say?" They'd spent the evening getting
reacquainted, our mother too. From the few facts Steve knew,
we invented a conversation in which Price recounted his departure from Haiti about 1971. By then there were troubles at
the Schweitzer. François Duvalier—"Papa Doc," Steve corrected me—was dead. From Port-de-Paix to Port-au-Prince the
roads were crumbling, sliding into the sea, and the sea was
dying around the islands. For money Baby Doc imported toxic
waste and dumped it inside the reefs.

As Price described each event, our father would have tried to
hold down his excitement. He'd sit forward on the living room
couch as he listened to the names of the places they'd traveled
together—Gonaïves, St.-Marc, Pétionville, Petit-Goâve—come
alive in Price's Creole accent. Now our father would have much
to contribute. He'd kept up all these years on what went on in
Haiti. He was something of an expert on the Duvaliers. Steve
and I argued that our father had always harbored a secret respect
for François Duvalier because he was an M.D. "But Duvalier
was a voodoo priest," Steve insisted. No doubt our father's
Christian heart took issue.

In fact Price had escorted our father to a vodun temple to
watch a series of rites performed. It was probably a commercial
gathering, the kind tourists could be admitted to. You paid a
fee to get in. Which of the rites they had witnessed we'd never
know for sure. At one point our father had simply ceased to

discuss it, and he no longer cared to be asked about it. Maybe Price had taken him to see the Rites of Rada, a ceremony often performed for foreigners which celebrates Haiti's connections with Africa. Price must have explained each part of the ceremony as the two of them stood in a sanctuary which by day might have served as an office or a shop, or someone's living room. Or maybe enough time had passed since the Revolution of 1957 that the meeting place was officially a temple, candlelit, full of true worshipers, the statuary set out on altars below pictures of the important spirits, Baron Samedi, Lord of the Cemeteries—whom the president was said to emulate in posture and dress—and Damballo Wedo, whose likeness is a serpent, along with the Virgin and a portrait of Duvalier himself on the walls.

Then our mother would have interrupted—it certainly belonged to their conversation—how she remembered Haiti, no matter how brief had been her stay. She'd gone to rescue our father, whom we hadn't heard from in weeks, and found him on her first stop, the Schweitzer, delirious with malaria. "He looked just awful," I imitated my mother's voice for my brother, but he didn't laugh. "She blamed Price, don't you think?" "Maybe—" Steve hesitated. "But she wouldn't have let on." "I bet she did," I said. "You *hope* she did," he said. "You're always after a little drama."

Now our father might have picked up the narrative, his manner suddenly terribly engaging. Say he stood and stretched, just as Steve did as he remembered our father's account of the night he knew the instant he was bitten. Yes, he knew it. No one could say otherwise, in spite of the drums and the dancing, the priest's chanting and the press of bodies around him. "Here in August," our father would say to Price, "you hear something like it in the orchard. Cicadas, tree toads . . . they sound like that little rattle. But I heard the mosquito," he'd insist, circling his left hand by his head. "I thought to myself, *I'll be!* See, I hadn't really been chewing those roots or nuts or whatever they were. I just pretended to." He'd bring his fist to his mouth and work his jaw to demonstrate the trick for Price.

This was a secret he'd kept from any Haitian. During the ceremony our father had been afraid to decline the nuts offered to him, and to everyone in the temple, for fear he'd be forced to eat them, nuts intended to induce in the onlookers and participants of the dance a mild trance. Maybe they were a version of the Vedic snakeroot, or they were simply a local seed treated with rum. "Na-a-a . . ." my brother imitated our father's voice, nearly challenging Price. "I faked you all," he'd conclude. "And I heard that mosquito." It was as if people had doubted him on this point over the years. "I tell you," he'd sit again, "I knew the moment I was bitten."

"How brave you were to come for him," Price might have said to our mother. Anyone would have tried to flatter her just then. She was tired, by now, of remembering. Or maybe the fear inherent in the memory had opened in her. Being afraid had always made our mother angry. "It's true for all of us," my brother defended her. "It's true for me," I agreed. "I've never been good at it. Some people are good at it. Some people are gracious even when they're afraid." "Not our family," said Steve. "But who, for instance?" "Well, like John Astor when the *Titanic* was going down. They say he put on a tuxedo and had a brandy." "That's not the same," said Steve. He was tired of the story, tired of my taking over, inventing details. Steve got up and prepared to leave the kitchen. "Look at it this way," he said as he walked out. "If Astor'd lived, he probably would have sued."

But the evening Andres Price passed with my parents in their living room couldn't have ended without my father's chronicling for him the decade following his own return to the States. "The worst," he'd say, "of my life. A terrible time." He'd speak for all of us. But he'd confess to Price that he'd held onto the drum, a vodun drum he'd carried back with him to Missouri in 1964. I saw that drum only a few times. A series of three drums is used in any number of vodun ceremonies. The *maman* is the largest, then the *seconde*, then the *cata*. I suspect my father's drum was a *seconde* or a *cata* because it was small, and made of a stained hide.

It was an object my father treated with respect and secrecy, like the conquistador's skull he'd once dug up in Mexico. He seemed ashamed and mystified by the drum and since he had no way of explaining it or justifying why he'd come to own it, he kept it locked in a trunk in the study off his bedroom. But some nights when he was feeling like himself, like traveling again or like a man who'd traveled, he'd bring out the drum and tell us his version of a story in which the dead were said to be raised.

He'd tap the head and bring his face down close to ours. "This drum," he'd whisper, "has seen it all . . ." As he spoke, our brothers put out their arms and wandered like sleepwalkers around my parents' bedroom. "Yes," chanted my father, "zombies, come out of your coffins. I have your souls . . . Here"— he'd offer the drum to us—"try it, girls . . ." We'd run for the door but we stopped there, hugging the frame. By now my brothers were going wild. They pulled at our nightgowns as they tried to drag us toward the drum. "Only Jesus can raise the dead!" we'd squeal. "You're right, darlings," our mother would answer her girls from her bed. Maybe she was reading her Bible or sewing on a button. "Out of the mouths of babes, Ev. Now stop that." The practical irritation in her voice, to our collective disappointment, broke the spell.

But my father blamed the drum for what he figured to be his

rotten luck through the rest of the sixties. For one thing, he'd tell Price, his health had failed. Was it the malaria? He couldn't say for sure. Now and then without warning he'd lose his appetite, feel heavy, tired, though he couldn't sleep for the ringing in his ears. And it was in the late sixties that his parents had become ill, both of them, with cancer. It hadn't been easy, feeling as he did, to look after them. No, there was no one else he trusted to do the surgeries. He wouldn't have considered it. He'd even built them a house on the east property line. Maybe my father took Price to the living room window and pointed to the lights through the trees. But his parents had been unhappy in Missouri. After they'd both recovered, they stayed a month, maybe two. Then they'd gone back East. He'd sold the house years ago.

And things had gone badly with the family. His daughters, as they grew, were trouble. The rows were endless. His wife cried every Sunday in church. By 1970, the four oldest girls were married, two still in their teens, out of school and married and pregnant. It was his fault. He knew it. He'd seen it coming when Rena turned her back on nursing, when Gena left her Christian college for the state university. "They grow up," my father would say. "They get pixilated. They have these crazy ideas. One told me she wanted to be an actress!"

As for the boys, they'd done all right at first, each one following my father through his alma maters, and every one of the four had become a surgeon, and later on, one of his daughters, too. But maybe because of the Vietnam War—Everett and Paul had to work in a government hospital for a while—or because of the way the medical profession was changing. The fact was not one of his sons had come back, as he'd hoped, to take over the practice in Missouri. No, the clinic was closed. He'd retired four years ago this spring, and locked the doors behind him.

Then an idea came to my father one night, maybe after a fight with one of his daughters or a late-night call from the hospital. Say one of his patients was doing poorly post-op. The nurses were worried or the family. The phone would wake Eva and me and we'd tiptoe to our parents' bedroom door. Someone was in pain. We could tell by the medicine he prescribed. Or someone was dying. "Tell the family to go home now," we'd hear our father say into the receiver, "there's nothing to be done. Here, let me speak to them . . ." Maybe it was an early spring evening in the year 1970, the first spring of a new decade, cold enough to wear a coat, yet the trees had blossomed. You felt it, that shifting, the jet stream moving down across the continent, the plains ridden by warmer air.

He'd taken the drum out of the trunk in his study, taken it out quietly so as not to wake my mother, and hidden it under his coat as he descended the main stairs, moved in the dark through the kitchen and out the back door. And say there was a moon so that he did not stumble as he followed the stone path past the fallout shelter and the rusting swing set, past the open yard worn bare in the shape of a baseball diamond beyond which were the hives, the barn. By the toolshed at the edge of the orchard where a row of forsythia had just finished blooming in front of the arbor that within weeks would be covered with yellow roses, he stuffed the drum into a mesh cylinder on top of the week's trash, stuffed it down hard, and threw a little gasoline on it and set it afire.

As for Andres Price, he'd spent the night in my parents' house. My mother probably made up the canopy bed for him in Eva's and my old room. The next morning my parents offered Price a job. They had no one these days to look after the clinic. They checked on it often, of course, but they worried about break-ins, vandalism. How about if Price took up residence in one of the outbuildings, the smokehouse, for instance? Once a bachelor teacher had lived there quite comfortably. The smokehouse had a kitchenette and shower. They could move some of the clinic's waiting room furniture in too, the roll-out couch, a table and chairs, whatever Price liked. He could be caretaker of the property, check the mail each day, keep the lawns mowed, the gardens tended, the flower boxes full. He could board for free.

Price accepted their offer. They spent the next few days settling him in. But in the end there was not enough work to keep him occupied. By late October the mums in the flower boxes had frozen. The mail was sparse. The sidewalks were swept clean by the wind. Andres Price began to wander around Jefferson City. Sometimes he'd disappear for a few days. Where did he go? My parents learned that he was taking meals at the Salvation Army. On the days my father went down to check on the clinic he might find the back door open. This was dangerous. He kept expensive equipment inside. He drove around town looking for Price.

Neighbors began calling. Who was this man? they'd ask. Was he a friend of the doctor's? At first the calls were polite. People, my mother would have said, just wanted to know. Later the callers aired suspicions. Why did the man wander around all day? He'd been seen on the highway, or on the bridge, or going through garbage cans in residential areas. "So what?" my father would have answered the citizens. Maybe he was having doubts about Price. Still, he would have defended him. But the man was wearing an IGA bag on his head, said one caller, a bag rolled up like a hat. "It's a habit," my father tried to explain. "They do that in the tropics. It's a cheap way to keep the sun off your head, or the rain. Clever, huh?" Say my mother took down to the clinic some of my brothers' old baseball caps. "But he looks funny," returned the caller. "He just grins when I say

something to him. He scares my kids, Doc. Where'd you say
he's from?"

One day Price was spotted on the empty street in front of the
clinic. The maples had lost their leaves and the leaves were
nothing, little shattered piles rising up suddenly in front of the
few cars in traffic, scaring the drivers. In the November light on
High Street Andres Price was said to have begun dancing. "I
reckon," said the witnesses, "he was a-tryin' to catch his
shadow. He kept a-steppin', a-jumpin' that a-way . . ." The
next time Price stopped by my parents' house he admitted he
was homesick. Maybe he could come back some spring when
the doctor really needed him, or if one of the boys came back.
Maybe some summer. That afternoon my father put Price on a
Greyhound bound for New York City.

CHAPTER 22   "*LILY, ROSEMARY, AND THE JACK OF HEARTS*"

During our seven years in Highland, I made many friends, but two, in particular, I was close to, so that when I remember California, I remember them. In fact it was Richard who introduced me to Trina in a creative writing class at the university, and Richard with whom I fought, many years later, over an incident following Trina's death. Trina and Richard wrote poetry. That was the only thing we had, at first, in common. I'd never heard of anything like a creative writing class, in which you actually got academic credit for writing poems. Nor had I ever shown my poems to anyone, except by way of the mail. I'd surmised that one was supposed to try to publish work because of the acknowledgments pages in the single volumes I loved best, *Life Studies, Ariel, The Far Field*. I copied down the names of the magazines listed in those books and I looked up their addresses in the Air Force base library.

In the beginning, I didn't know you were to enclose a self-addressed stamped envelope, but the magazines answered me nevertheless. Howard Moss of *The New Yorker* politely mentioned the return envelope. I was thrilled to see his handwriting, to receive such a handsome rejection slip. I couldn't believe that he—and all the others—had bothered to answer me, to communicate, by way of folding my poems again, neatly, and replacing them in the envelope, enclosing such pretty forms. And they kept coming, rejection slips from *Harper's, Chelsea, The Atlantic Monthly, Poetry,* with now and then a little comment. "Too elliptical," said one. I laughed out loud in my happiness. Such a comment implied that someone had actually read the work. He hadn't questioned whether it was poetry. He'd assumed it was, and had an opinion on it *as* poetry. But what did that mean, *elliptical?* I looked up the word in the dictionary. "Obscure, incomplete constructions," it said. Right, I agreed. OK. No more Plath for a while. No more tercets, incomplete sentences. I'd work on *elliptical.*

I saved the rejection slips in a folder which I kept in my kitchen drawer, the ones with handwritten notes on top. They gave me courage, and after a year in Highland, I applied to the University of California at Riverside, applied there, particularly, because the university offered the military and their families in-state tuition. Riverside was, by Missouri standards, some distance from us, about a thirty-minute commute, one way. But once I was accepted, little Charlie and I took the drive as an adventure, stopping, mornings, for doughnuts before we pulled onto the freeway. I'd enrolled him in the day-care center on the UCR campus rather than the one at Norton because I wanted to have him close to me, especially when Charlie was out in the system.

Maybe those drives to Riverside initiated in little Charlie what would become his keen sense of direction. At first, I often got us lost. The freeway's ten lanes across and steep overpasses scared me. Sometimes I'd panic and take an exit that did not feed back onto the interstate for miles. Or in my elation at passing a truck while we sang to the radio, all the windows of our red Volkswagen bug rolled down, I'd pass up the Riverside exit and we'd be on our way to San Diego. "Not yet, Mom," little Charlie would instruct me when, suddenly befuddled, I'd put the turn signal on for the wrong exit. "Two more to go. Slow down. You're over the speed limit." He would turn four in May. We began classes at UCR in the winter of 1974.

In a creative writing class you come to know maybe more than you'd like, and quickly, about the other students. Richard was clearly a veteran of the workshop, which I understood to be an extension of previous workshops. You could take the course repeatedly for credit. Richard wrote close-up, present-tense poems that found their way in tight syllabics down the page. They began bizarrely, often surreally. He read them to the class, then sat back, staring down at the floor until the discussion, praising or damning, concluded. He was a big, handsome, sad man, his face now and then giving up to humor, in which case he'd smile and meet your eyes. The suggestions the class made concerning revision of his poems he'd nod to, but he never, as I came to find out, changed a thing. Richard had written hundreds of poems, which he kept in a folder, each poem immaculately typed, hugging the left margin, untitled, and he refused to capitalize a single word.

Trina monitored and mothered Richard, and by mid-term she'd taken me on as well. "Let me handle it," she liked to say. During poetry class, for instance, she'd act as a sort of interpreter of the criticism Richard's and my poems received. If she disagreed with the comments, she'd reach across the table, lay her hand over our copies, and shake her head. If the comments were, in her estimation, way off the mark, she'd laugh out loud and swear. It always surprised me to hear her do so. Trina looked much younger than she was—about twenty-one when I first met her—and her colorful expressions, "Well, fuck my mother's

little beagle dog," or "Eat me last week, honey," didn't seem
to belong to her blond countenance, her freckled, boyish face.
"Excuse me, Miss Barnett?" the instructor would say after one
of Trina's outbursts. Then she'd simply put her head down on
her arms and remain that way for the rest of the class, snickering
to herself, until she fell asleep. On the other hand, when her
poems came up for discussion, she listened hard and took many
notes, shrugging off Richard's and my attempts to console her.
Later she'd take us to task. We'd usually seen her poems before
she'd presented them to the workshop. "They were right," she'd
snarl over coffee in the Commons, "this one's full of clichés,
and *you* didn't see it. What'sa matter? You need glasses?" Trina
had a variety of questions with which she'd answer "What'sa
matter?" depending on the circumstance. "Your arms broken?"
"Your mother didn't love you?" and "You think you're the frog
prince?" were just a few.

At first I thought that Richard and Trina were lovers, but as
it turned out, they were simply friends who'd met a few years
back in the ongoing poetry class. Trina had a list of incompletes
that kept her, for most of the time I knew her in California,
from graduating. Richard, who was a little older than I, was
working on a graduate degree in Comparative Literature. He
lived in San Bernardino with his mother. Besides going to
school, Trina worked as a cook in a home for juvenile delin-
quents. She kept her own apartment in Riverside in which, to
make ends meet, she raised mice and sold them by the hundreds
to laboratories and pet shops. One Christmas she made a gift
of one gray male and one white female to little Charlie. "See
if you get a spotted one," she told him. "And you better separate
them before long, or she'll eat the babies." She put her hands
over little Charlie's ears and addressed me, "Bad for the kid's
psyche."

As the term progressed, and the next, Richard and Trina began coming over to Highland in the evenings when Charlie was away, and sometimes when he wasn't. I'd cook them dinner and we'd read one another's poems or listen to music. A station out of Los Angeles I particularly liked because, along with the hourly news, it reported the nautical weather, when to expect high and low tides, the height of the Pacific swells, and offered warnings on all-clears to fishermen. Maybe the reports helped me to place myself on the continent. And though I hadn't yet seen the Pacific, I liked to imagine it out there, vast and exotic, over which, in- or out-bound, Charlie flew. The station was called Coast and it broadcast Muzak twenty-four hours a day. The first time they visited, Trina and Richard eyed each other over the cheap renditions of "Misty," and "Am I Blue?" but they said nothing. To them I was an anachronism, a married woman—an Air Force wife, in fact—with a four-year-old child. Pinehurst Village, with its Corvettes in the carports, its mothers walking babies in strollers, its identical stucco facades on which the windows slid sideways, its sprinkler systems that, on a timer, we often watched come on at one, then again at four a.m., was to them a novelty, in its way, an anesthetic in context to their lives.

One night, as I labored, with poor results, over a recipe out of *The Joy of Cooking*, Trina took the book from me. "Let me see that thing," she said. She'd brought cherry brandy for our dessert but she'd opened the bottle when she saw me getting out pots and pans. She studied carefully the illustrations in the cookbook—how to sharpen knives, cut up a side of beef, set a table, roll out dough. Then she turned to the calorie chart. I waited for her to make fun. Trina and Richard had awakened in me an old desire. I seemed to be trying my hand again as a home economics expert. They believed, because I cared for a child, had a husband, owned property, that I must be naturally domestic. I didn't want to disappoint them, even when they teased me. But instead of making fun, Trina looked earnestly up at me. She had a beautiful face, large eyes and pale brows. "For years," she said, "I wondered what a *lactating* woman was. I thought it was like *Amazon* or *Lesbian* . . . like someone with her own river, her own island. *Lac*-tating," she repeated slowly, "*lac*-tating . . ."

When it got late, Trina liked to tell Richard and me about the most exciting accidents she'd had in her car on the freeways— she'd had many—or about the time a few years back when, unable to pay her rent, she'd prostituted herself in L.A. By the one a.m. sprinklers, she and I had usually had a lot to drink, and as my questions turned more and more explicit, Richard would stand solemnly, prepared to leave. "Siddown." Trina would grab his arm and pull him into his chair. For a moment, he'd resist. "OK, OK." She'd relent. "We'll clean it up. Just let me say this. Three digits, honey." She'd hold up her fingers in front of my face. "Three." In fact, Richard never said much those evenings, but Trina and I learned not to let him withdraw from us completely for fear he might, as we'd say to each other alone, "go under."

When he became what Trina and I considered too quiet those evenings at my dining room table, we'd try to draw him out by gossiping about my neighbors in Pinehurst Village. For some reason it was a subject that reassured him. "I should tell you"—I'd lean toward them like a conspirator—"that the other evening, *that* one"—I'd point to the wall behind me—"stumbled over here—didn't I tell you this?—with a big cut on the side of his head. 'My God!' I said, '*Joe*,' I said, 'what happened?' He was still wearing his flight suit. It was covered in blood. I guess he'd just gotten home from a trip. You remember Joe, Richard. He's the guy who talked to you that day about Jesus, remember? The one whose wife doesn't speak English . . ." Richard smiled weakly. "*That* guy . . ." he said. Trina kicked me under the table. "Anyway, I got him a cold rag, you know, and sat him down. He looked real pale. I said, 'Put your head between your legs, Joe,' but then I was afraid he'd bleed on the carpet!" "Deborah!" Richard came to life. Trina winked. "I said, 'Maybe you need to go to the hospital, Joe.' 'No, no,' he said. 'Just let me sit here a minute.' I offered him a drink but he said he just wanted water. Made a point of it. He's quit drinking, since he—you know—since he converted.

"Well, in a few minutes, here comes Toy." "Who?" Richard was engaged now. Trina sat back, satisfied. "Toy. That's his wife. Remember? I told you about her. Joe married her in Thailand. They had a Buddhist ceremony, but after Joe got born again, he made them say their vows to the chaplain. He blabbed to everyone at the wedding that he and Toy had been *living in sin*. Toy didn't know what he was talking about!" "Poor kid," said Trina and winked at me. "Really," I agreed. "Anyway, in a minute, here she comes to the back door. She's looking real upset. 'Come on in,' I said. 'Joe's hurt.' I knew she knew it, but I didn't know what to say. Then I saw what she had in her hand! It was one of those little mallets you use to soften meat!

" 'Don't let her in,' Joe says when he sees it! I sort of jumped in front of her. 'Give me that,' I said to Toy. It was crazy! 'Now give it here . . .' I always shout when I talk to her, as if she were deaf. She looked at me like I was nuts. I tried to take the mallet from her but she ran. 'Should I go after her?' I said to Joe. I stuck my head out the door and watched her run along the wall. She jumped over it at the playground. 'She's gone over the wall!' I said to Joe. He just sat there so I closed the door again. I got him some more water and made an ice pack out of a dish towel. I kept watching the yard. 'She's been gambling again,' was all he said, 'but I'm not giving her any more money and that's that. She can beat me to death but I'm not giving her any more . . .' Apparently she's been going up to Victorville when he's away." "How?" Richard sat forward. "She got her driver's license somehow. Studied the book and took the test and passed." "That's wild." Richard got up and went to the screen. If the sprinklers were on, he'd close the glass panel. "You know your floor gets wet if you leave this open?" He was back with us. Trina poured herself another drink. "What about the ones"—he gestured to the right wall—"over here?"

Trina and Richard attended the parties I threw for little Charlie, brought him gifts, and sang "Happy Birthday" with me on cue. Richard often accompanied me to do shopping at the base, though because he had no military I.D., he had to wait in the car. They watched, one afternoon, as I lay down five bags of steer manure out of which I hoped to coax a lawn. They helped me shovel it into the sand, seed it, and celebrated with me at the first weak dusting of green. One fire season a pair of peafowl appeared on our back patio and Trina and I fed them bread crumbs, set out coffee tins full of water, and when they flew up to light on the wall, Trina took my photograph as I crouched in front of them. It's a funny picture. I have my hair in rollers anticipating, I imagine, Charlie's arrival. The male peacock looks like a cutout. It must be February or March. Behind the birds you can see snowcapped mountains.

By then Trina was living with someone in Palm Desert, a man she claimed she loved but who, she'd admit, "doesn't give a goddamn what I do." On weekends she'd drive in and stay with little Charlie and me. We'd go for long drives through the orange groves, stopping, now and then, to investigate the many abandoned houses hidden deep in the orchards, beautiful old places that seemed to have been empty a long time before they'd either been rented out or simply inhabited by drifters in the sixties. Sometimes the doors were locked, but the windows, without panes, we climbed through. "I'll go first," Trina insisted as I made a ladder of my hands and hoisted her up over the sill. Little Charlie and I'd wait until she returned with an all-clear. "Give him to me." Trina would reach through the opening and lift Charlie in.

We tore rock posters and war slogans and electrical tape peace symbols from the walls of what became our favorite house, a two-story Victorian, off a dirt road near Redlands, surrounded on three sides by trees. It was full of junk which we spent one afternoon piling out back, evaluating, as we worked, any salvageable pieces, an aluminum deck chair, some sofa cushions, motorcycle parts. "That's a carburetor," Trina pointed out to little Charlie. "You want it?" It had occurred to Trina recently that she might join the Army. She fancied herself going in as a mechanic, and she'd cut her hair short, like a man's. "I'd learn a little discipline," she'd explain. "I'd have to get up in the morning, be on time to work, or . . ." She'd draw her hand, like a blade, across her throat. It was true Trina was inevitably and hopelessly late to anything, to work, to her classes, to my house. She'd lost job after job because of it.

It was dangerous to climb the stairs of the Redlands house. Some were missing and the others gave a bit each time we went up, though from the second-story bedroom window you had a wonderful view of the orchards that stretched for several miles toward the foothills. That room had wallpaper of delicate flowers, and Trina and I walked off where we imagined the bed had been, the dressers, the mirror. "It must have smelled just like this," she'd said, leaning out against the sill. The neglected orchard still bloomed, though the fruit, when it came, was blighted, the skins like a bright orange leather. We found a stockpile of smudge pots on the back porch, most of them rusted through, but Trina put together the working parts of several pots, threaded a wick, and bought kerosene. "Now we can stay past dark," she said. Once or twice we coaxed Richard to our house in Redlands. Having stopped by the drive-thru at McDonald's, we sat on the porch and had a picnic. Little Charlie was fascinated with our smudge pot and he could hardly wait to light it. Neither could Richard. He didn't like the house much, and when the sun went down, it was pitch black among the trees, the sky toward the freeways an eerie yellow. Besides, Richard saw the house as it was, trashed, abandoned, beyond repair. "It's probably haunted," he'd say, so that we didn't stay long when he was with us.

CHAPTER 23 *NEW YEAR'S*

On the way home from Riverside one afternoon I stopped the car at a gas station. I barely made it to the ladies' room before I was suddenly, violently ill. "I guess I got the flu," I said to Trina when I returned a few minutes later. "I'll drive," she said. I handed over the keys. "It's funny, though," I said. "I feel just fine now." As it turned out, I was pregnant, and I was happy about the news. It was something I'd wanted, something which for the last year I'd become obsessed with, I can't say exactly why. I'm afraid it had little to do with Charlie, though the trouble we'd experienced during our first two years in California—even filing once for divorce—seemed behind us.

I'd written the courts myself to explain our change of heart. "Differences reconciled," I'd said in a letter and sent it off to Riverside Courthouse, on whose steps I had turned to Charlie some months before. "We had wedding pictures," I insisted bitterly. "Here—" I'd handed him our camera. "Take mine, then I'll take yours." We laughed over those pictures later. I haven't seen them in years. Maybe Charlie has them, or maybe we threw them away. As for his absences, I'd gotten used to them. I even looked forward to having our rooms to myself again, having the nights to myself to write, or study. I finished my degree in 1975 and went on to graduate school. Or I'd complete a project: brick the kitchen or wallpaper a room.

In the summers little Charlie could stay up as late as he wanted. While I worked he liked to direct, in front of the mirror, "The 1812 Overture," because of the drums and cannon fire. Sometimes we played it so loud on the stereo, our neighbors would appear at our front door. They'd knocked on the walls. They'd called us on the phone, but we couldn't hear it ringing. They threatened to call the police, but they never did, and after a while, little Charlie moved on to Strauss.

Trina was by turns curious about, maternal toward, and suspicious of my pregnancy. My fatigue made her impatient, and the fact that I wouldn't drink or smoke anymore, and that red meat made me ill. "How 'bout a nice juicy steak?" She'd eye me evenings as I prepared our dinner. I'd taken to making tomato aspic from a recipe out of *The Joy of Cooking.* "Rabbit food," she'd complain as I set the aspic, shimmering from the mold, in front of her. Later, though, she'd produce books she'd checked out from the UCR library which showed the fetal stages of development. "Comere," she'd say to Richard and little Charlie. They'd sit on the couch on either side of her while she turned the pages. "See?" she'd observe. "Your mom's about here." She pointed to the fifth month. "It's in its monkey stage," noted little Charlie. Trina whooped and hugged him. Richard chuckled too, but politely. The whole thing made him nervous.

"I think you should lay it out in spades," Trina advised me, one afternoon, concerning how specific I should be in telling little Charlie about conception and birth. "Just come clean. That stork business is bullshit." "I never considered the stork," I said.

We were sitting, as usual, at my dining room table. I'd just cut out a pattern for a maternity blouse. Trina had helped me pick out the material. Like my sister Eva, she had a knack for sewing. We'd rented a Singer for a week. "But he's only six," I said. "He's a smart six," Trina returned. "He can take it. Look, I'll do it if you want to. I saw this book, see. It's written for kids . . . Here, let me do that." Trina began removing the pins from the cloth. "I think this is a good color for you." She held the pieces up to herself. "Just let me handle it." She lay her hand on her own flat belly. And sure enough, a few nights later, she brought over a present, as she often did, for little Charlie, and the two of us took him through it. "Now why don't you draw about it?" she suggested after we'd read him the book. "Draw a sperm with your name on it swimming up toward that little island. Remember this, kid. You're a born winner. You won the race to the egg."

I was in my ninth month when Trina told me about her pregnancy. I hadn't heard from her in several weeks, so that when her car pulled up out front, I went out to greet her. It was a typically hot day in early October. The Santa Ana winds had just come through, and after months of the smog haze, the clarity hurt your eyes. I was barefoot. The brick path burned my feet and I hopped from one to another. "Stop that," she barked at me, "you're going to fuck yourself up." Trina looked pale and angry. It was unlike her to go without makeup. Her face looked bloated. Below her halter top I saw she couldn't button her jeans. "I guess I meant to," she told me after we'd unloaded her things from the car. "I mean, it was sort of an accident, but I let it happen. It seemed like fun, I guess." She looked me over and shifted on the chair. "Jeff's furious. He doesn't want it. S'cuse me." She leaped up and ran to the bathroom. I tried to go in but she held the door. "Don't," she called. She ran the water high, but I heard her retching. "Some coach I'll be," she said when she emerged. "Don't worry about it." I set a glass of ice water on the kitchen counter. Trina had trained with me, as they called it, to be my Lamaze coach in the event that Charlie was away during the baby's birth. She'd gone with me, over the last months, to the natural childbirth classes at San Bernardino General Hospital. It was a calling she'd taken so seriously, I half hoped Charlie would be away. Trina braced herself over the sink. "How's the kid?" she asked. "Which one?" I tried to joke. "This one"—she pointed to my belly. "Wild," I said. "I can't sleep anymore . . ." I resisted the temptation to take her hand, as I often did, and place it on the spot where the baby was kicking. "Listen," she said, suddenly straightening. "I don't think I'll stay, after all. I gotta talk to Jeff some more . . ." "Call him up," I said. "Maybe it would be good to talk at a distance." "He'll just hang up," said Trina. "Or he's probably not even there . . ."

"I took my own advice." I spoke to Trina later that night over the phone. She'd returned to Palm Desert. She was alone. "I mean," I said, "the way I look seems to contradict what I'm about to say, you know?" Trina snorted. "Whatever you do," I said, "it's OK with me. You don't need my permission." I felt my face burn as I spoke. Trina and I never talked to each other this way. "Is Charlie home?" she asked suspiciously. "He's supposed to be in sometime tonight. If you have it, or if you . . ." "You can't even say it," Trina exploded. I figured she'd been drinking. "Give me a break," I said. "You know what I mean." "I'll handle it," she said, but more softly. "I don't know what I was thinking." "Nobody ever does." "I just think if I don't have it, I'll never get another chance." "That's not so," I cooed. I sounded like my mother. "Look at me, all of seven years later. It's just hormones talking . . ." "Jeff's back," she lied, "I gotta go. Listen—'' She paused. ''Good luck,'' she said. ''OK,'' I said, ''you too, and let me—'' ''Gotta go,'' she interrupted, and hung up the phone.

I didn't hear from Trina again until about three months after Stephen was born. It was New Year's Eve, 1978, and I'd invited her and Richard for dinner, but Trina was late, and after a couple of hours, we'd gone ahead and eaten. I was upstairs with the baby when the doorbell rang. Trina had brought a friend. ''This is Alex,'' she called up to me where I stood on the landing. Richard had come into the living room and he shook Alex's hand. ''I'm glad you left Jeff,'' I said to her later as we stood over the baby's cradle. ''Cute little fucker,'' Trina spoke loudly. ''This thing rock?'' She shook the sides of the cradle until the baby stirred. ''I just got him to sleep,'' I said. ''He's a lot fussier than Charlie was.'' ''Jeff moved months ago.'' She shook the cradle a last time and stepped away. ''Now it's Alex.''

Trina sat down on the edge of my bed. ''What do you think of him?'' ''Interesting.'' I hesitated. Trina laughed. ''Don't let the leather jacket fool you,'' she said. ''He doesn't even own a bike. I guess Richard told you about the abortion,'' she said suddenly. ''He told me,'' I said. ''How do you feel?'' ''Never better. See?'' Trina stood and pulled up her blouse. ''Lost a little weight,'' she said. ''Jesus, did I put on weight but quick.'' ''Do I know.'' I tried to sound sisterly. ''Just look at me.''

Trina stood back and took me in. I looked terrible. I was at least ten pounds overweight, my hair was dirty, and I had the baby's spit-up all over the front of my shirt. I waited for her to take a crack at me. I saw it taking shape in her eyes. But after a moment she said, ''You look fine.'' She sniffed the air. ''Smell great, too.'' I laughed and began to unbutton my shirt. ''I know,'' I said. ''It generally smells like shit in here.'' I tossed the milk-sour shirt in her direction. Suddenly it felt good to be changing in front of her and I didn't turn away. She stared at my breasts, red and streaked from the stretch marks, the ugly maternity bra, the fat roll of my waist, my jeans, unbuttoned and unzipped. I moved slowly. I wanted her to look at me. Maybe I thought she'd be glad of what she'd missed and pity me, take over things again. Or maybe I just wanted a witness —another woman—to register my condition, to say, if only by way of an expression, "I see."

I put on one of Charlie's shirts. "Let's go down," I said. I felt happy, closer to her now. "Richard's been acting kind of weird . . ." "We can't stay." Trina slapped her thighs and stood. "No?" I couldn't hide my disappointment. "Alex and I got this idea to raise tropical fish." She checked herself in the mirror. "You know, breed 'em, sell 'em. He says he knows of a fish pond in front of one of those big hotels in Palm Springs. They just let them swim free. We figured we'd snag us a few while everyone's inside partying, take 'em home and see what happens." "How do you know the males from the females?" I asked. "Details." She slapped my back and held onto my shoulders as we descended the stairs.

It was the last time I ever saw her, though about a year later, she called me from California. By then Charlie and the boys and I had moved back to Missouri. It was as if we'd driven backwards through the seasons. The January day we left Highland it was seventy-five degrees and sunny. By Oklahoma the wind blew so fiercely, trucks were overturned on the shoulders. We made Missouri on the fourth day, just before a snowstorm. It happened that Trina called one October evening in 1979. I remember precisely because it was Stephen's second birthday. My parents had driven up to Columbia to celebrate with us, and several of my brothers and sisters. My parents had made the trip to try, as my father said, to help Charlie and me "work things out. You have family here," he'd plead, then launch into a story about troubles he and my mother had had in their marriage. There was a certain elation in his tone since, only a year before, fed up with caring for my father's mother—a stern, recently widowed Dutch woman—my mother had actually left my father. My sister Rena had called me in California. "By any chance," she'd asked, "is Mother there?" I'd laughed out loud. Mother? In California? "It's no joke," Rena reprimanded me. "She's left Daddy. We can't find her." "Try the lake house," I'd advised. "We did." Rena was upset. "We can't get an answer." "Maybe she's not answering the phone," I suggested. "Don't worry. Mom's all right. She just doesn't want to be found right now. You know Mom. Mom's fine," I assured her. In fact, the lake house was where Mother had gone.

When the phone rang during Stevie's party, I was glad for the diversion. I took the extension in the kitchen. "Look," said Trina when I explained, "it's OK. I'm leaving in a few minutes, anyway. I was just thinking about you." "I hate this," I said. "They're waiting for me to bring in the cake. Can I call you later?" We hadn't spoken in a long time and I was anxious to talk to her, to tell her about Missouri, the difficulties Charlie was having adjusting to a nine-to-five routine, the difficulties I was having with it. "Call me tomorrow," said Trina, "same number. Not too early," she reminded me. The phone rang the next morning near eleven, about eight o'clock California time. I heard the static that meant this was long distance, and a voice, so like Trina's, said, "Hello?" "You're up with the birds." I laughed. There was a silence. "Trina?" "No," said the voice, "this is Trina's mother. Is this Deborah?" and so on. Trina's mother described the accident Trina'd had on the freeway the evening before. "She crossed the median. It was a head-on. They assure us she didn't suffer." Trina's mother caught her breath. "People say she wasn't watching. They say she was combing her hair . . ."

Not long after Trina was killed, UCR called to invite me to a memorial ceremony they were planning in Trina's honor. "Anything's better than that circus they called a funeral," Richard greeted me at the Ontario airport. I hadn't seen or heard from him in over a year. "Can you believe it?" he said. "They buried her as a *Mormon*." But the university ceremony couldn't, I decided afterward, have been much better. It had been haphazardly planned. A few people—some of Trina's old professors, students from the poetry class, her mother and father—milled around the classroom in which the reading was to take place. In the month following the accident, students who cared to were supposed to have written her an elegy. Most of the students hadn't seen Trina for years. She'd had words with many of the professors over extension after extension of her incompletes. One by one we read our flaccid, morbid attempts. The reading dragged on for hours.

Richard, who was angry with Trina's parents because of the nature of her funeral, read one of Trina's poems in which she chronicled, in great detail, her pregnancy and abortion. It was not one of her best attempts. I imagined she must have enclosed it with a letter as she often did when she wrote Richard or me from the desert. Later she might write again to say, "The poems I sent were shit." That Richard read Trina's poem that afternoon made me furious. Grief does strange things to people. People like Richard dive into it and swim out into the deep water until someone comes and gets them, or until they arrive on the other side. Grief made me righteous, like someone calling instructions from the shoreline after the swimmer. Unheeded, I turned bitter, and I railed at him the next morning as he drove me to the airport. He met my tirade with silence. I got out of the car while it was still moving and slammed the door.

We didn't speak again until years later. In 1987 I flew from

Boston to Riverside to do a poetry reading. My first book of poems had just been published and UCR had arranged to bring me out to California. Much had happened since the last time I'd seen Richard. Charlie and I had been divorced in 1980, nearly a year to the day after Trina died. Since then I'd lived in Seattle, Iowa City, London, Washington, D.C., and recently Boston, where I taught writing at a university. Little Charlie, who insisted on being called Charles now, was seventeen, a junior in high school. Stevie was ten. And I had remarried.

Richard and I apologized to each other and reminisced. I told Richard about the recurrent dreams I'd had after Trina's accident in which she would call me on the phone. He'd had the same dreams. "The last one I remember," I said, "she was sitting on the edge of my bed in Missouri." Richard and I had just ordered hamburgers in the Bob's Big Boy near campus. He hadn't changed much in appearance. I think I believed that after I left California and Trina died he'd be lost. In fact the opposite had happened. He'd gotten stronger, made new friends. He looked well, more handsome than I remembered. He still lived in San Bernardino with his mother, but now he worked in a hospital. He'd all but stopped writing poems.

"She was wearing a nightgown," I continued, "the one we picked out at May Company for me to put on right after Stevie's birth. Were you with us? It was red, of all things, remember?" "I remember." He smiled. " 'Hey,' she said to me, 'I've been waiting for you. You're very late.' " Richard laughed at the reversals. "She didn't say it, but I knew she wanted me to come with her. 'I've got the house fixed up,' she said. I knew she meant the one in Redlands. 'I can't,' I said. 'I want to but I can't. I can't leave the boys.' 'Why not?' she said, and then I realized there was no way to make her understand." Richard smiled and nodded. He'd always been good at sympathy. He

knew how to get out of the way of people's feelings, like taking
care not to step on another's shadow. He didn't try, as I always
did, to fix things, and I was suddenly, overwhelmingly sorry
I'd never, in nine years, called or written.

When we'd finished our burgers, Richard, at my request,
drove me around a little. We took the freeway to Highland and
I peeked over the fence of our old carport to see the redwood
deck, still intact, still sturdy, which Charlie and I had built years
ago. It occurred to me to call Charlie when I got back to Boston
and say so, though I never did. The field behind our condominium had been developed and many ski lodge–type apart-
ments stood in rows all the way to the foothills, though the
planes took off and landed, as always, to the east. Toward the
desert the orange groves had disappeared and roads crossed and
intersected so that I couldn't quite get my bearings as to where
we were. Neither Richard nor I mentioned trying to find the
house in Redlands.

"People want to give you a party," Richard told me as we
headed back to Riverside, "you know, to celebrate the publi-
cation of your book." "I have to get back tonight," I lied. "Didn't
I tell you? In fact"—I glanced at my watch—"if we could drop
by the motel, I'll just pick up my things and check out." Richard
didn't argue and I understood that he was relieved not to have
to escort me to the party. "You know what Milton said after
my reading?" I laughed. Milton Miller had been my creative
writing teacher at UCR. "He said I should have stuck to fiction."
"Are you sure there's a flight?" Richard seemed not to have
heard me. "I'll just get to L.A. and go from there." I tried to
sound worldly.

I'd already made a reservation, though I knew I'd be penalized
a hundred dollars for changing my ticket. Initially I'd had great
hopes about my trip to California. I'd packed summer dresses,

even my swimsuit. I'd imagined sitting out by the hotel pool, talking with my old friends about writing, anxious to hear about their work over the last ten years, anxious to tell them about mine. But nothing had gone according to plan. For starters the pool just outside my hotel room was being renovated. I'd checked in to the sound of jackhammers tearing up the concrete. As for my friends and teachers, the ones, that is, who hadn't moved away, they'd given up writing. And in some odd way —as intimidating to me as the searing sunlight, the great distances between exits on the freeway—none of them appeared to have aged. In our surprisingly polite exchanges of the day before, after my reading, I'd felt terrifically self-conscious of the gray in my hair, the lines around my eyes. I sensed, no doubt wrongly, that they expected a story from me, a story of my travails, which, looking into their smooth, untroubled faces, I decided to refuse them. As Richard and I drove toward the Ontario airport, I felt shame and embarrassment at what had turned out to be my own sentimental expectations of the trip.

We parked the car and Richard carried my suitcases inside. We hugged and promised to keep in touch. We didn't mean it, but we had enough respect for each other to go through the motions. We said we'd write. We'd call. "Shall I wait until your plane takes off?" Richard asked. "No, no," I insisted. "You can't go to the departure lounge anyway. That's something new, isn't it, since the last time? Send me some poems," I said as we loaded my bags on the conveyor belt. "Do you have my book?" I asked. "I'm ashamed to say I don't." Richard smiled. "I don't get out much." I grabbed my luggage off the belt and took out a copy of my new book of poems. "Take this one," I said. "It's all marked up. It's my reading copy—I make notes on the poems, see. I get so nervous when I read I forget what I want to say . . ." A line of people waiting to go through security was forming behind me, but I took another moment to reach into my purse and pull out a pen. Richard held the book open and I signed my name on the title page. "Do you still write?" I asked. "Not much," he said. "Sometimes." We hugged again before I entered the security check. "I'll send some poems to you," he called. "Do that," I called back from the other side of the doorway. "Promise?" Richard moved over to the partition and put his hand against the glass. "I will," he mouthed, "I promise."

CHAPTER *24* *FUGITIVE SPRING*

The only time my mother ever left my father, she'd just turned sixty-five and she fled, as she would tell it, to our lake house in the Ozarks. She escaped in mid-March when there's still a raw cold in the air. Dirty snow lingers in the shadows of the houses, and in the backyards all that was mercifully covered—dilapidated lawn chairs and rusty shovels and faded plastic pools dusted at the watermark with a gray moss —lies exposed on the brown grass like studies in neglect. Under the bald spring sun, under maples and sycamores still leafless, everything looks pocked, eroded. The women in their husbands' boots move about the yards, scooping up what they can in their aprons and piling the rest next to a garage or cellar, their bare arms chill-mottled, their hands red and cracking. It's the time in Missouri when you realize how you've aged. Even the light softened through bathroom windows reveals frankly the brown spots along your cheekbones, or in profile, the slackening neck. But you turn on the mirror, assess the damages, and dry your hands. Hanging the wash out for the first time this season you know what's irreparable, or considering at the back door the longer light one evening, what can be saved.

Our lake house was built of wood almost black from years of my father and brothers' spraying its exteriors with linseed oil and creosote to protect it from insects, and each of the windows wore a pair of forest-green shutters. It was the last residence on a winding gravel road whose descent leveled off into a small peninsula, the road down the hill banked on either side by many varieties of oak and hickory and maple and pine trees, and redbuds, too, the smaller ones close to the road tagged with faded ribbons during this or that spring when my father's ambition to transplant them peaked. He'd cruise the tree line during one of his cabin checks and single out the saplings, visible by their early blossoming, and tie up branches with one of our hair ribbons which we wore always at the ends of our braids. But the time he did try to move a redbud, it died within a season and he'd bent his shovels too. It had been a messy, miserable job. He'd butchered the roots that would not come away clean, the soil in the Ozarks being rocky, a black to orange gravel out of which jut small bluffs of chalk and sandstone scored with red clay.

Grass grew sparsely, even in the warmest months, giving the area the appearance of arrested spring. You must wear shoes in the lake region, yet there were times when departing from Jefferson City for a month-long stay, we'd forget our shoes and so wear rubber thongs all summer—even to church—which my mother bought at the bait shop, but we went barefoot most of the time, the thongs broken or carried out into the channel. To get to our cabin you passed through a woods canopy until you broke into the open. Where the land sloped gradually to meet the lake stood our place, the first house on the shore were you to approach it by water. My mother arrived there at dusk without her purse, the keys to the cabin, a change of clothes. At that time the lake's a darker version of the sky and the only thing moving out on the surface is a duck or two or one of the locals in a rowboat with his flashlight on as he sets out for a night of frogging.

The Lake of the Ozarks is man-made, a huge area of hills and farms flooded in the thirties by surrounding rivers, and no matter how many new docks over the years jutted out from its shore, drive-in motels and craft shops filled with cedar products—plaques and jewelry boxes with *Lake of the Ozarks* burned into their surfaces—Indian souvenir stores, and later, go-cart tracks and water slides, the lake retained always the aspect of its original, vast burial, owing to its steep banks and the debris that would surface now and then when the water through the Bagnall Dam was emptied or filled. Barn siding or sawhorses or stock mangers bobbed into our cove just under the water, each piece moss-black, eerie, authentic, and heavier than we could have imagined before we dragged it like an artifact onto our dock, where it dried a stinking gray-green under a cloud of flies. When the coast guard horn sounded some early September morning signaling that the body of the lost fisherman or the missing child had been found, or on the contrary, when no horn sounded and the fleet returned with its dragging hooks suspended to some government dock up-lake, you could imagine, as if from some light-layered view distorted through the lens of the water, rooms down there.

Our cabin was built soon after the flooding by a man named Cook who retired there to live another twenty years. When we moved in in the early fifties to spend our first summer there, the cabin was furnished down to linens and dishes. I remember several sets of shot glasses, which were foreign to us since our parents didn't drink and which we loved for their size and fought over until we'd broken every one. Cook had decorated the living room walls himself with cattails which he'd strung near the ceiling. Over these he'd hung about fifty plaster geese in an autumnal scene, but as time went on, the seed masses exploded and the damp, dead matter began to attract fleas and gnats, so that my mother took to emptying a can of Raid on it every so often. She insisted that Cook's last efforts at artistic expression be preserved.

The place was an odd conglomerate, rooms that opened onto one another and each onto a screened-in porch that, supported on stilts over an embankment, wrapped around two sides of the cabin. The basement rooms, tucked into the hillside, always smelled of mildew. Cook's game room included an elaborate pool table which my father converted into a tool table, ruining intentionally, it would seem, the massive hand-carved mahogany legs, the way he tried out his saws on them. In the ball pockets he stored his hammers and screwdrivers, picks and wedges. Early on he'd confiscated the pool cues, since my brothers had immediately appropriated them as swords and fenced wildly around the cabin and my mother feared someone would lose an eye. The balls also disappeared because we couldn't help but want to throw them.

My mother broke easily into the cabin that evening, removing the electrical tape that patched a rusty screen and shattering the pane near the window lock. As she raised the sash, I think she must have remembered how in the early sixties during an exceptionally cold winter a stranger had broken into the cabin to stay a couple of weeks or so. We suspected he lived on squirrels.

Apparently he'd found the fuse boxes and the water pump. The bathtub showed a grim watermark, and in the kitchen sink a single cup and saucer sat neatly washed, but they'd cracked from the cold. Some of our army blankets were tangled on the bare mattress in my parents' bedroom and one of the feather pillows still held the indentation of a head. That summer we scrubbed the place down like never before, but after the intruder the cabin took on eerie proportions, its many closets incorporated into our frequent nightmares, its winter emptiness haunting the brightest summer days, as if we'd been witness to the break-in, to the bone-cracking sounds of the ice shifting on the lake, echoing the thud of the hatchet.

Whether my mother suspected it or not, she was not the second, maybe not even the third person to let herself into the cabin by other than the front door. Some years before, when I'd been eighteen and in love, I'd lied to my parents, telling them I was staying the night with a girlfriend. Then my boyfriend and I drove the forty-five miles from Jefferson City to the lake in his father's car, parked up the hill, and sneaked down to unmask the same torn screen, shatter, against my friend's football letter jacket, the same pane, and slip in the window. It was dark or nearly dark by the time my mother heaved herself over the sill and stood in the center of the living room, the stuffed eagle with the stuffed mouse in its beak, the owl, and other effigies professing to Cook's amateur attempts at taxidermy looking down at her from each of the walls. I imagine her standing in the twilight, unafraid, crossing her arms as she anticipated her next move.

More than twenty years after birthing her last child, my mother carried the residual weight of ten pregnancies. Nearly six feet tall, she stood erect, a healthy woman—save bouts with high blood pressure—and she looked to be, at most, in her early fifties. She kept her hair dark brown and she swept it up high in a French roll with stray wisps—set each morning with a curling iron—framing her face. At sixty-five she was handsome, powerful; her strong Dutch features: a large straight nose, thick brows, and deep-set blue eyes that looked directly into your eyes as she leaned slightly forward, forehead down, sharpened her expression. When she was angry her eyes were terrifying; she'd raise her right brow high as an old sea captain's. Like my father she had a quick temper. Unlike him her anger knew no self-consciousness. Her wrath, as it found a voice, revealed some high-minded interpretation of broached loyalty or morality, and she gave in to preserving at any cost the appearance of things, even in the face of chaos. Among ten children, for instance, there's discord, but we were never allowed to fight around her or swear or, most of all, speak indiscreetly to friends about what went on in our house. She had no patience with any kind of cruelty or self-indulgence.

She was suspicious of any sexual airs, especially on the part of her daughters. When I was about thirteen, I borrowed a friend's Johnny Mathis album and played it over and over on our Mickey Mouse record player. I mooned around the room, trying on my sisters' pretty underwear as I took stock of my body. My mother caught me in the act of stuffing bobby socks in the oversized bra I wore as I swung my hips toward the mirror. She dropped her load of clean laundry, grabbed me by the arm as though she were snatching me from the path of an oncoming car, and slapped me. Then she ripped the record off the turntable and broke it over her knee. She hated closed doors, secrecy, which she perceived as deception, and she could quote numerous Bible verses about sex, coming from the Old Testament.

Yet she was generous, big-boned and ample-bodied, not especially modest, often dressing and undressing in front of us as she dusted herself with talc and whisked her hair up, pins in her mouth, turned her face left and right, quickly, happily evaluating her efforts. She loved bright lipstick and nail polish which she bought from the Avon lady, and she wore broad-brimmed hats which she kept in a box under her bed, replacing the flowers each spring with new ones from Woolworth's, and she let us try them on whenever we wanted. She always wore dresses and stockings and she pinned real flowers from her overgrown gardens in her and her baby girls' hair every morning of the summer, dabbed perfume on our wrists and gave us, when we asked for them, Tony home permanents.

I must have suspected that afternoon in my thirteenth year that my mother's actions weren't her own. They seemed to belong to some notion she had—and had failed in her own mind—of Christian purity, and I've never held them against her, not that day or on any other when she tried to quell my sisters' and my passions. I think I sensed, even with my cheek burning, that she wished she were someone else, maybe one of the cold, pale women from our church, who wore beltless dresses and shamed young girls with clicking noises and frowns. I have a picture of her my father took one morning. She's asleep, her beautiful big mouth slightly open. Beside her are three children under four years old. She's probably pregnant. On the nightstand three baby bottles sit atop her Bible. The clock reads six a.m. She'd wake each morning to dirty diapers, dishes, meals to cook, fights, accidents, injuries, the ninth month coming ten times in her life, the ninth month—whatever she believed—meaning that there was less and less time to play the piano or garden or sing in the church choir. Certainly she'd never feel again, except when lifting two babies at once, the tightness in

214

her thighs from having executed a high kick when she danced with the Rockettes in her twenties.

At sixty-five my mother in high-heeled shoes felt her way along the wall down the stairs to the lake house fuse box and water pump, felt her way as our intruder had, or her sixth child, this daughter, with my first lover. Then we'd stripped in the dark in a basement room and made sudden love on the damp bed, the creaking pipes against the dead spring silence startling us who leapt up, sure we were caught, and listened, and lay down again, laughing, nervous, surprised to tears at what our bodies could do without instruction. My mother stayed, at most, a couple of weeks at the cabin, from late March to early April, the trees transforming around her, the days getting warmer. She lived on the money she received by returning Nehi and Pepsi bottles, an accumulated twenty years' worth, which she systematically loaded into the trunk of the car and delivered to the tiny grocery on the highway. She got a nickel a bottle and bought food with the money—bologna, bread, eggs, and coffee. Carl, the longtime owner, must have been surprised to see her hauling case after case to his counter. The other residences on our road were still closed up, it being so early in the season. And what did she wear each day? The only clothes at the cabin besides sweatshirts and swimsuits were her old maternity dresses.

She had set herself up in the cabin's big kitchen, had dragged one of the army cots in from the porch. The lake house had no heat. She'd kept warm by lighting the gas stove, turning it up to broil, and opening the door. During the afternoons, as the weather grew warmer, she might take a walk along the shore or sit out on the dock reading old *Woman's Day* magazines or *Ladies' Home Journals*, especially the "Can This Marriage Be

Saved?" articles, some of them dating back to the early fifties. She'd forgotten her Bible, but she came to realize how much she'd memorized and wrote down some of her favorite verses: Romans 8:28—"And we know that all things work together for good to them that love God, to them who are the called according to His purpose"; and Philippians 4:8—"if there be any virtue, and if there be any praise, think on these things"; and others which she displayed on the refrigerator.

I can imagine my mother in some faded muumuu sitting in an aluminum deck chair on the paint-stripped dock in early April, her hair pulled neatly back, her cheeks bright from the afternoon sun. From there she could watch the trees across the cove take on foliage, the first dusting of pale green deepening, filling in the twiggy shadows above the shallows where the crappie eggs hatched among sunken tree limbs and the huge carp that ate the shoreline garbage swung their bright tails in and out of the sunlight. All of her children were grown by that spring, the last one almost finished with college. Maybe she could hear in the distance the buzz saws lopping off dead branches distinguishable now among the leaves, hear the first pleasure boats setting out for a day on the lake, their air horns blaring the first bars of "Never on Sunday." Across her lap, maybe a magazine lay open to a woman in the latest fashion. Mother was given to cutting out ads from Saks and Bonwit Teller in which the models, she claimed, looked like her own daughters.

Say a wind came up off the lake and it grew chilly and so she made her way back up the steep stone steps to the cabin to prepare a little supper. My mother stayed until it looked like summer and she could plant plastic geraniums in all the window boxes, do some weeding around the rose of Sharon, sweep the patio clean of dead leaves, until one evening, her supply of soda bottles exhausted, her food store gone, she changed into her street clothes, taped up the torn screen, climbed back out the window and closed it behind her. Then she drove home to take up the task again of caring for my father's recently widowed mother.

CHAPTER *25* *INTERNATIONAL WATERS*

For my twenty-fifth birthday, Charlie bought me a lesson in a glider. We drove toward Laguna Beach to the airfield, and Charlie and little Charlie watched me climb, behind the instructor, into the tiny cockpit. A tow rope connected us to a lead plane. As soon as we were strapped in and secure, the lead plane took off in front of us and in a moment, we, too, were airborne, heading for the open fields. Beyond the fields were the cliffs along the ocean that caught the off-sea winds and produced strong thermals by which we'd navigate, once we were cut free. It was February and you could see a long way. Only a hint of smog ceilinged the basin, and the mountains had taken on a green-blue aspect. From that height I thought I understood how centuries ago those mountains had been pushed up from the earth, the desert tumbling away from them. Through decades of rain and wind loose earth must have caught in the crevices and many varieties of seeds, which had been carried for miles, perhaps years, by the Santa Anas, took root and grew. Now, where the rock faces pitched at an angle, those seeds had become a wall of trees. As we swung out behind the lead plane and climbed, the sun grazed a wing and we were shot through with light. The instructor handed me some goggles.

They reminded me of the X-ray goggles my father used to wear at the clinic. I could go days now without thinking of my family, the house on Main Street, the orchard. Then, as if to chide myself, I'd dream everyone back, or dream myself back to Missouri. "Then we which are alive *and* remain shall be caught up together," wrote Saint Paul, "to meet the Lord in the air." Sometimes I existed whole days under the hood of those dreams. I'd call my sisters. Eva lived in Florida now, Rena in Illinois, Gena in Minnesota. Or I'd call home. "It's below zero," my father would report, his voice grim, a tone I recognized and shrank from. I'd put Charlie on and he'd converse with my father about the frozen pipes, the "sheet of ice" that was the driveway. As he listened, Charlie would grin widely and point to the hummingbirds swarming our feeders. When he hung up the phone, we'd actually jump up and down, dance, laughing, around the kitchen as if, in spite of his constant comings and goings and the troubles we had, we were glad we had escaped—had we *escaped?* In the beginning we hadn't known to call it that—Missouri.

"Now don't be afraid," the instructor warned me. "When we let go of the lead, there's a pop." In preparation, he began identifying for me the various controls, the stick that operated the elevators, the wings, the tail. "Listen," I said. "I'll probably never do this again. Could we just ride? I like to listen to the wind. It's my birthday," I added. "It's your nickel." He smiled. I peeled off the goggles and my eyes adjusted to the brightness. Suddenly I wished that, of all people, my mother could see what I saw. I almost heard her voice as she sang out greetings or last-minute instructions. All families have their own peculiar talents. Mine has always been good at big send-offs, no matter what the crisis has been or its outcome, everyone outside, everyone in the driveway waving good-bye.

But like those dreams I still have, dreams like all-night parties, crowded with brothers and sisters—we're all in the kitchen, pots and pans knocking in the sink, or we're piling into the car on our way somewhere, to church, to the lake, to the St. Louis Zoo where one of us, inevitably, will be left, missed halfway home, turned around for, retrieved and celebrated—dreams from which I wake alone in Seattle, or Iowa City, or London, or Washington, or Boston, happy it's not the past, the pilot cut the tracer and we drifted free.

"What's that?" I pointed out in front of us. "That's the Pacific," laughed the instructor. "Here—" He played with the stick and we turned out toward the water. A thermal caught us and we were lifted high. I saw beyond the cliffs the flat, hazy expanse, the sun on the far surfaces erasing its color. "We'll have to head back in a minute," he said, "the winds are light today." Our shadow swept the hills. Charlie and little Charlie waited for me somewhere on the ground. That night we'd probably have a party. Trina and Richard would be there. My parents would call, and some of my sisters, to wish me a happy birthday. I'd tell them about the glider ride. My father would say, "You're a quarter of a century now," and we'd laugh. We both knew my mother had briefed him, before the call, on my exact age. "Have your presents arrived?" my mother would ask from the downstairs extension. "Not yet," I'd answer. She'd sigh. "The mail's so slow to California." What she meant was that she'd forgotten. She'd send something out tomorrow, or the next day, or the next.

When it got late, Charlie would excuse himself and he and little Charlie would go on up to bed. Trina, Richard, and I would sit up a while longer, gossiping, listening to Coast, finishing off the wine and the cake. I looked behind me out the glider's porthole window as long as I could. From that distance, the Pacific might be any ocean, the green curve of the shallows finding blue-black depths. I seemed to remember it, and the way the land must have looked upon approach, maybe because Charlie had described it to me so many times, or my father by way of his father who, as a boy, had watched the New York City skyline take shape from the fourth-class deck of a steamer. The instructor maneuvered the craft so that we seemed to turn on an axis and the horizon cut the window nearly in half. At that moment I'd never be farther away from Missouri. To look across the water was to look somehow toward home.

A NOTE ON THE TYPE

This book was set in a typeface called Méridien, a classic roman designed by Adrian Frutiger for the French type foundry Deberny et Peignot in 1957. Adrian Frutiger was born in Interlaken, Switzerland, in 1928 and studied type design there and at the Kunstgewerbeschule in Zurich. In 1953 he moved to Paris, where he joined Deberny et Peignot as a member of the design staff. Méridien, as well as his other typeface of world renown, Univers, was created for the Lumitype photoset machine.

Composed by PennSet Inc., Bloomsburg, Pennsylvania

Printed and bound by The Haddon Craftsmen, Inc., Scranton, Pennsylvania

Designed by Harry Ford